Quaff 2008

PETER FORRESTAL is a freelance wine writer who lives in Perth – 'Some of the time', grumbles his beagle, Fling. He is the wine columnist for *STM* (the local *Sunday Times Magazine*) and for *The Bulletin*, and contributes regularly to *Australian Gourmet Traveller WINE*, the *Qantas Magazine* and *Money Magazine*. He writes the Australian entries for the *Oz Clarke Pocket Wine Book* and contributed to the sixth edition of Hugh Johnson and Jancis Robinson's *The World Atlas of Wine*. Peter continues to talk about wine with Madeleine Randall and John Clarke on ABC Statewide in NSW and appeared in two episodes of the ABC's television almanac *Can We Help You?* He is in his tenth year as chairman of judges for *Gourmet Traveller WINE*'s Winemaker of the Year Awards and has just become chairman of judges for Fine Wine Partners' Australian Wine List of the Year Awards.

He was founding editor of *Australian Gourmet Traveller WINE*, and is the author, co-author or editor of 30 books, including the *Global Encyclopedia of Wine, Discover Australia: Wineries, and Margaret River*. In 2007, he judged at the International Sweet Wine Challenge, the Riverina Show, the Qantas Mount Barker Wine Show of Western Australia, and the Perth Hills Wine Show. Peter is a member of the Circle of Wine Writers (UK) and FIJEV, the International Federation of Wine & Spirits Journalists & Writers.

Quaff 2008

Peter Forrestal

Hardie Grant Books

Published in 2007
by Hardie Grant Books
85 High Street
Prahran, Victoria 3181, Australia
www.hardiegrant.com.au

All rights reserved. No part of this publication may be reproduced, stored in a retrieval system or transmitted in any form by any means, electronic, mechanical, photocopying, recording or otherwise, without the prior written permission of the publishers and copyright holders.

The moral right of the author has been asserted.

Copyright © Peter Forrestal 2007

ISBN 978 1 74066 530 8

Edited by Clare Coney
Text design by Phil Campbell
Typeset by Prowling Tiger Press
Printed and bound in Australia by Griffin Press

1 3 5 7 9 10 8 6 4 2

For JC (John Clarke)
who retired from the ABC earlier this year and is now working harder than ever for them (difficult though that may be for him to believe). We have shared conversations about wine over ABC Statewide on his Sunday morning program for the past five years – with John in Newcastle and me chatting from Perth (occasionally), Paris, Margaret River, the Mornington Peninsula, the Barossa ...

Remembering the fun and JC's vivacity, wild enthusiasm, savoir faire and joie de vivre

and for his tolerant Margaret

and David, Emma, Andrew and all those lucky grandchildren.

Contents

ACKNOWLEDGEMENTS	x
BARGAIN HUNTER'S SURVIVAL GUIDE –	
AN INTRODUCTION TO BUYING GREAT-VALUE WINES	1
Top 20 Quaffing Wines of 2008	4
The Quaff 2008 Awards	5
Hall of Fame: The Reliables	8
How This Book Works	9
Vintage Reports: 2007–2002	12
FOR A PLEASANT DAILY DROP –	
TRY THE BEST CASK WINES ON THE MARKET	15
White Casks	20
Pink Casks	24
Red Casks	25
Fortified Casks	28
MORE FROTH THAN BUBBLE – SPARKLING WINES UNDER $15	31
White Sparkling	36
Pink Sparkling	41
Red Sparkling	42
Sweet Sparkling	44

BOTTLED SUNSHINE – WHITE WINES UNDER $15	47
Chardonnay	50
Riesling	60
Sauvignon Blanc	65
Semillon	70
Other White Varietals	74
Semillon Sauvignon Blanc Blends	80
Other White Blends	88
BLUSHING BEAUTIES – PINK WINES UNDER $15	95
Pink Wines under $15	96
BARBECUE WINES – RED WINES UNDER $15	103
Cabernet Sauvignon	106
Merlot	114
Shiraz	118
Other Red Varietals	129
Cabernet Merlot Blends	134
Grenache Blends	139
Shiraz Cabernet Blends	143
Other Red Blends	147
THE HONEY WIND BLOWS – SWEET WINES UNDER $15	151
Sweet Wines	154
Sweet Reds	155
Very Sweet Wines	156

UNFASHIONABLE BUT STILL GREAT –	
AUSSIES FORTIFIED WINES UNDER $15	157
Port	161
Sherry	164
Muscat and Tokay	165
THE FOREIGN LEGION – IMPORTED WINES UNDER $20	167
Imported Sparkling	171
Imported Whites	173
Imported Rosés	177
Imported Reds	179
LASH OUT – GREAT-VALUE WINES OVER $15	183
Sparkling Wines over $15	186
White Wines over $15	187
Pink Wines over $15	197
Red Wines over $15	198
Sweet Wines and Fortifieds over $15	209
HOW TO TRACK DOWN THE BARGAINS	213
Some Tips for the Bargain Hunter	215
Finding the Wines	217
Recommended Retailers	230
Wine Clubs and Online Retailers	245
DECODING THE JARGON – A QUICK WINE GLOSSARY	247
INDEX OF WINES	253

Acknowledgements

No one but Claire Codrington could stem the deluge of tasting samples that flood the office as another edition of *Quaff* comes upon us, unless it were our newest recruit, Nicole Milne. A lesser woman than Nicole would stare at the scene and mutter, 'I don't believe this'. Fortunately, Nicole just gets on with it quietly.

Proximity to the action and her kind heart means that Elaine Forrestal is called on quite often enough – and, for that and much more (washing the bottle hiders and destaining the table cloths), I am deeply appreciative.

Nevile Phillips hasn't improved. Nor has he got any worse (except when the Eagles lose). He is model of consistency and a tyrannically efficient chairman of the tasting panel whose support I treasure. I also acknowledge the camaraderie of Nevile and colleagues Mike Adonis, John Jens, Diana Loots, Will Nairn, Wendy Roach, Natalie Schaefer and Max Veenhuyzen around the tasting table at 1 Cobb Street. We all look forward to welcoming Nicole Walton back from maternity leave and meeting Mitchell.

I also acknowledge the support of wine producers and wholesalers who, by supplying samples of their wines, provide the foundation on which the book has been built. Our contacts at these wine companies have been unfailing cooperative and have frequently gone far beyond the call of duty.

In the spirit of the *Quaff* Awards, we announce that Rebecca Bunyan and Robyn Clasohm are sharing the 2008 'Dot the i's'

Award for efficiency. With staff changeovers, things have been more than a little difficult at Hardys, and Rebecca and Robyn have been super-helpful. The Reliables: Alex McPherson has been with us for all eight editions of *Quaff* and Margot De Bortoli and Paul Lenon have helped with seven of the eight editions. Paul Lenon is handing over the hard work to Melissa Milani and so, before he disappears from the radar, Claire is keen to award him our long-service 'Codrington Medal' for having made her life so much easier over so many years.

We would also like to make a fuss over the following for their cheerful hard work on our behalf: Andrew Anderson, Bev Atkinson, Leah Baker, Mark Bolton, Paul Boulden, Rebecca Bunyan, Robyn Clasohm, Bel Darley, Kate Davey, Margot De Bortoli, Jeannie Duhigg, Claire Ellen, Hayley Dunn, Michelle Hall, Tim Hodgkinson, Alice McGillivray, Tracey McIlwain, Jayne McKennay, Alex McPherson, Lloyd Meredith, Melissa Milani, Tiffany Nugan, Kristen Pryce, Matt Redin, Melanie Routledge, Julia Rowse, Andy Salmond, Natalie Schaefer, Nitzan Schell, Jeremy Stockman, Fiona Tiller, Paul Tyers, Katherine Ward, Emily White and Sally Wiltshire.

I am deeply appreciative of the support, encouragement and quiet calm of those at our publisher, Hardie Grant Books; particularly Jasmin Chua, whose efficiency and gentle manner brings out an author's sense of guilt better than anything. The support of Julie Pinkham and the return of Clare Coney (and her young border collie Toby) make my life as an author much easier. And in Clare's case, makes me appear a much more presentable author: thanks for the invisible mending. I also love the work of Fran Berry, Keiran Rogers, Jenny Macmillan and website maestro, Greg 'Arv' Arvidsson, and acknowledge the contribution that they make to the success of the book.

Elaine Forrestal continues to be calm, tolerant, supportive and loving, while the manic extreme youth of the popular beagle, Fling, is a distant memory as he hits the threes. He now provides moments of light relief and comradeship in his never-ending pursuit of yet another pat. His stunt of almost choking on a bone on deadline day took attention-seeking to another level.

Bargain hunter's survival guide

An introduction to buying great-value wines

INTRODUCTION

PETER FORRESTAL

There's little doubt that the 2007 vintage will be remembered in Australia as the harvest which broke the glut. In most parts of Australia, drought, bushfires, hail and frost conspired to wreak havoc on the grape harvest. Yields dropped dramatically for 2007 (and are likely to remain low for 2008 as well) so that the surplus of wine, which had kept prices low, became a thing of the past. It seems that prices will rise to more sustainable levels as grape-growers and winemakers have suffered from the low prices of the past few years. Already, in scanning through your favourite large company wines, you'll see prices have gone up a few dollars. There will still be discounting but you can expect to pay more for your wines over the next few years.

    The good news for lovers of *Quaff* is that there is still huge choice in the under-$15 price range – and I've be able to exceed with ease my target of 400 decent quaffing wines under $15. The best of these are as good as ever – perhaps even better than ever. It's been eight years now that we've published *Quaff* without having to compromise and raise the price point of the book. I'm certain it's possible to do this again next year and my target is to push things along so that in its tenth edition *Quaff* can still proudly single out the best wines under $15.

The retail trade continues to be worth following as Woolworths and Coles continue their expansionist plans. The independents may well be having to work harder but they seem to me to be doing a good job offering an alternative to the supermarket chains. I'm impressed by the work that Vintage Cellars and Dan Murphys are doing with value-for-money imports. Our imported wine chapter has never been so comprehensive.

The number of subscribers to the *Quaff* website has gone up by 50% in the past year suggesting that bargain-hunter wine lovers enjoy up-to-the-minute information. I have been reviewing my Wine of the Week, plus another bargain each week so that (free) subscribers are aware of any exceptionally good bargains as soon as they come onto the market. *Quaff* is now the first annual wine guide to remain up to date all year round. There are plans to upgrade the site and I'm looking forward to working on that.

We conduct the tastings later in the year than any other wine guide and cover more of the new season's wines than anyone else. However, there are plenty of companies that haven't yet released their 2007 whites or 2006 reds. The *Quaff* website will keep you informed as the best of them hits the market. The focus is on wines at the *Quaff* price point with the occasional gem that is just over $15. If you aren't already a subscriber, join up now – it's free at **www.quaff.com.au**. You will receive an email each week to alert you to the new bargains that have been posted on the website. Get your friends and colleagues to enrol too. Quaff on!

TOP 20 QUAFFING WINES OF 2008

Something new in *Quaff* this year. We thought our readers would enjoy my ranking of the best of the best under $15: the top 'Bloody Goods' (in order) from *Quaff 2008*:

1. 2007 Peter Lehmann Eden Valley Riesling
2. 2006 Yalumba 'Y Series' Shiraz Viognier
3. 2006 De Bortoli 'Windy Peak' Pinot Noir
4. 2005 Capel Vale 'Debut' Merlot
5. 2005 De Bortoli 'Deen Vat 5' Botrytis Semillon
6. 2007 Jim Barry Watervale Riesling
7. 2006 Schild Estate Grenache Mataro Shiraz
8. 2007 Primo Estate 'La Biondina' Colombard Sauvignon Blanc
9. 2005 Ferngrove 'Symbols' Cabernet Merlot
10. 2007 Brown Brothers 'Zibibbo'
11. 2006 Red Knot Shiraz
12. 2006 Yalumba 'Y Series' Shiraz
13. 2006 Angove's 'Nine Vines' Viognier
14. 2006 Jacob's Creek 'Three Vines' Shiraz Grenache Sangiovese
15. 2007 Ferngrove 'Symbols' Sauvignon Blanc Semillon
16. 2007 Sandalford 'Element' Classic White
17. 2006 Water Wheel 'Memsie' Shiraz Cabernet Malbec
18. 2005 Coriole 'Contour 4' Sangiovese Shiraz
19. 2006 Angove's 'Long Row' Cabernet Sauvignon
20. 2007 Innocent Bystander Moscato

Just missed:
2006 Angove's 'Long Row' Chardonnay
Banrock Station 'Reserve' Sparkling Shiraz
Morris 'Black Label' Liqueur Muscat
De Bortoli Show Liqueur Muscat

A DRUM ROLL PLEASE ... IT'S THE QUAFF AWARDS

The Quaff 2008 Awards

These are the standout wines from the *Quaff* tastings; they represent superlative quality and exceptional value for money.

THE 2008 OBERON KANT AWARD FOR
THE QUINTESSENTIAL QUAFFER,
THE ULTIMATE AUSTRALIAN WINE UNDER $15 and
THE QUAFF 2008 'Whooshable'
WHITE WINE OF THE YEAR AWARD

2007 Peter Lehmann Eden Valley Riesling

Peter Lehmann Wines has done consistently well in *Quaff* over the years. Perhaps its most consistently good (or even great) performer has been the Eden Valley Riesling. This is the fourth consecutive year in which it has been rated 'Bloody Good'. One thing that I love about the wine is its fresh vibrance in its youth and its ability to age gracefully. The 2007 is breathtakingly good: fragrant, pure, fine and delicious. Against worthy opposition, it's the *Quaff 2008* Ultimate Australian Wine under $15.

THE QUAFF 2008 'Platinum Pillow'
CASK WINE OF THE YEAR AWARD

Hardys 'Reserve' Cabernet Sauvignon
(See page 25.)

THE QUAFF 2008 'You Can Launch My Ship'
SPARKLING WINE OF THE YEAR AWARD

2007 Brown Brothers 'Zibibbo'
(See page 44.)

THE QUAFF 2008 'Baubles, Bubbles and Beads'
BEST SPARKLING UNDER $10 AWARD

Banrock Station Sparkling Pinot Noir Chardonnay

(See page 36.)

THE QUAFF 2008 'The Gluggable'
BEST WHITE WINE UNDER $10 AWARD

2006 Angove's 'Long Row' Chardonnay

(See page 55.)

THE QUAFF 2008 'Run for the Roses'
PINK WINE OF THE YEAR AWARD

2006 Jacob's Creek 'Three Vines' Shiraz Grenache Sangiovese

(See page 99.)

THE QUAFF 2008 'Fillet Steak and Chips'
RED WINE OF THE YEAR AWARD

2006 Yalumba 'Y Series' Shiraz Viognier

(See page 124.)

THE QUAFF 2008 'Sausages and Chips'
BEST RED WINE UNDER $10 AWARD

2006 Angove's 'Long Row' Cabernet Sauvignon

(See page 108.)

THE QUAFF 2008 'Any Port In a Storm'
FORTIFIED WINE OF THE YEAR AWARD

Morris 'Black Label' Liqueur Muscat

(See page 165 .)

THE QUAFF 2008 'A Foreign Affair'
EXOTIC WHITE WINE OF THE YEAR AWARD

2007 Giesen Sauvignon Blanc

(See page 173.)

THE QUAFF 2008 'Another Foreign Affair'
EXOTIC RED WINE OF THE YEAR AWARD

2005 Portone Valpolicella
(See page 180.)

THE QUAFF 2008 'For They Are Jolly Good Chaps'
WINERY OF THE YEAR AWARD

Angove's
The Riverland's family winery, Angove's, is the deserved winner of our Winery of the Year Award although they faced tough competition from Yalumba and last year's winner, De Bortoli. The improvements at Angove's were evident last year but the quality of the wines has continued to get better and their performance over the past twelve months has been exemplary. From 25 wines submitted, 20 have been featured in *Quaff 2008*: nine of those have rated as 'Bloody Good' and five as 'Good'. It's been great to see the lift in quality with both the table wines and fortifieds.

THE QUAFF 2008 'Move Over Darling'
BEST NEW LABEL AWARD

Capel Vale 'Debut'
No question about the winner of this award: Capel Vale for its 'Debut' range with six wines featured in *Quaff 2008*: 'Bloody Goods' for their Chenin Blanc, Merlot and Cabernet Merlot and 'Good' for their Shiraz. Capel Vale is owned by Peter and Elizabeth Pratten who run the winery with their son, Simon. They are based at Capel and have vineyards in Geographe, the Great Southern, Margaret River and Pemberton. Consultant winemaker Larry Cherubino has been a huge influence – and obviously they have a terrific winemaking and viticultural team.

HALL OF FAME: THE RELIABLES

After eight years of sniffing and slurping through thousands of wine for *Quaff*, there are a few that have never failed to impress. The list is slowly reducing in size. However, those which remain have been recommended in every edition, regardless of vintage or label change. *Quaff* salutes the Reliables.

Sparkling
Banrock Station Pinot Noir Chardonnay
Banrock Station 'Reserve' Sparkling Shiraz

White
McWilliam's 'Hanwood' Chardonnay
Moondah Brook Verdelho
Primo Estate 'La Biondina' Colombard Sauvignon Blanc
Rosemount Estate 'Diamond Cellars' Semillon Chardonnay
Tahbilk Marsanne
Westend 'Richland' Sauvignon Blanc

Red
Bleasdale Malbec
Peter Lehmann Shiraz Grenache
Rosemount Estate 'Diamond Label' Shiraz

Sweet and Fortified
Brown Brothers Lexia
Penfolds 'Club' Tawny
Penfolds 'Club Reserve' Aged Tawny

You'll find these among the lists of consistent performers in each chapter under the heading: 'The reliables – consistent-quality wines, year in, year out'.

HOW THIS BOOK WORKS

So, what do we mean by good value?

Value means tasting – or drinking – a wine, enjoying it immensely, finding out the price and then saying to yourself: **'Bloody hell, does it really ONLY cost that much?'**

It's being happy to pay more for a wine than you actually paid. It's then – to a certain extent – gaining more enjoyment from that wine because you know you paid a reasonable price for it.

Value is relative, of course. There are plenty of $5 wines that are overpriced, just as there are $50 wines that provide just as much pleasure as wines three or four times the price. This is an important point: good value doesn't mean cheap. In recognition of this, a whole section of the book has been dedicated to wines over $15 – wines that I reckon offer exceptional value.

But I still believe that **most wine bought in Australia for everyday consumption is still under $15 a bottle**. In fact, about 90% of wine bought in Australia costs less than $15 a bottle. This is certainly where the most dramatic discounting happens in the larger stores. And if you take into account that 50% of all wine sales are casks, then the average price comes down to significantly less than $15 per 750 ml of wine. So the majority of wines recommended in this book are still under $15.

The low-yielding 2007 vintage and the likelihood of the 2008 harvest also having below-average yields has meant an end to the glut and a gradual rise in prices. There is little doubt that prices will increase over the next year or two and it will be harder to find the kind of bargains we've become used to over the past three or four years. However, I believe that with the help of this annual guide and the weekly updates on the *Quaff* website that you will still be able to find plenty of exceptional wines for less than $15.

How the wines were chosen

To start with, I approached all the major (and many smaller) wine companies in Australia, and asked them to submit samples of their under-$15 wines for tasting – as long as they would be available commercially from October 2007 until at least the end of the year. Importers were asked to submit wines under $20. I was still receiving and tasting these wines right into August, which means that I was able to evaluate many, many 2007 vintage whites and 2006 reds (even a few 2007 reds) before they hit the retail shelves.

This means that *Quaff* contains more recommendations for wines you can actually go out and buy than any other wine guide.

The wines were all tasted blind – that is, I had no idea of the identity of the wine in the glass in front of me. In my view, this is the only fair way to assess wine: having even the slightest glimpse of the label, or a peek at a distinctive bottle shape, will influence the most determined taster. As always happens, I encountered some surprises: wines with big reputations that tasted very ordinary, and wines that I didn't expect to perform well coming up trumps on the tasting bench.

This year I have included more wines with a recommended retail price above $15 than I usually do. This only occurs when the wineries or distributors insist that the wines will be readily available on special for less than $15 or when I've found this to be the case. When this occurs, I will make the recommended price clear to you.

The list of great-value wines over $15 was compiled from the extensive tastings I do as part of my everyday job as a wine writer. Those selected are the best value offerings of the last 12 months. I have been assured that they'll be commercially available at the time of publication and until at least January.

A unique rating system

Some wines are better than others. So, within each chapter on the wines under $15, my selections have been grouped under three headings:

BLOODY GOOD – a delicious example of the style that over-delivers on quality and offers great value

GOOD – above-average example of the style that offers good value

PRETTY GOOD – if you're in the local drive-in bottle shop these are the reliable wines you can count on to provide a nice drink.

So while I can recommend about 40% of all the under $15 wines I tried, I'd only rate about 10% of them 'Bloody Good' – and 60% of the wines tasted I'd happily drive past in that bottle shop rather than drink again (a harsh but fair image).

I've tried to make the tasting notes as informative, easy to read and evocative as possible. The often confusing, technical wine language has been kept to a minimum.

Reading the entries

The reviews are placed within each chapter under the three headings – 'Bloody Good', 'Good' and 'Pretty Good'. In each case, they are in alphabetical order of the wineries from which they come or the brands under which they are sold. In the index wineries such as Peter Lehmann, Geoff Merrill and Jim Barry are listed in alphabetical order according to the family name of the company.

How much is it, and where can I get it?

These are possibly the two most important questions for a wine drinker. And only one of them is easy to answer.

How much is it? When I asked the wine companies to tell us how much their wine cost, they gave me a suggested retail price based on the wholesale price, plus tax, plus retailer mark-up. But the wine trade in Australia is a dynamic and fluctuating beast, with discounting, local retail patterns and various behind-the-scenes deals and promotions all leading to sometimes quite fluid pricing. So while I can offer the suggested retail price as a guide, you may find that the price on the shelf in your favourite store is different – it will hopefully be lower, but it may be higher.

You will also notice a few wines in the under-$15 chapters with a full suggested retail price of over $15; we've done this with wines that will be widely and regularly available for less on discount, and made it very clear how much you should be able to find each wine for if you shop around.

Where can you get it? Under-$15 wines tend to be produced in fairly large quantities, so we feel confident in saying that, unless otherwise stipulated, you should be able to find most of them at most bottleshops, fairly easily. Exceptions are self-explanatory: if a wine is only available through one retail chain or direct sales operation, for example, we have indicated that. But to help get you started on the road to discovery – and to finding the less widely available over-$15 wines – we have also included (starting on page 217) contact information for the distributors of all the wines, and listed recommended retailers in each state and territory.

Finally, all wines mentioned (apart from the casks, of course), are 750 ml bottles, unless otherwise specified.

VINTAGE REPORTS: 2007–2002

2007
For much of Australia, 2007 was a very difficult vintage. Drought, frost, hail, bushfires and poor fruit set in much of eastern Australia caused drastically reduced yields – down by almost 30% from 1.85 million tonnes in 2006 to 1.34 million tonnes in 2007. While the production of whites fell by 17%, that of red wine was down by nearly 40%. Cool-climate regions, except Tasmania, were decimated, with production dropping by an average of 45%. Unseasonal weather meant that 2007 was one of the earliest vintages on record – from two to six weeks ahead of expectation. Fortunately for followers of *Quaff*, good rainfall in January, which helped the vines get through to harvest in better-than-expected condition, meant that the warmer regions of the Riverland and the Murray Darling did particularly well: their reds could well be exceptional. The other areas to defy the trend and experience very good vintages were the Hunter Valley and Western Australia, where many believe that 2007 could be the best harvest ever.

2006
The 2006 harvest was slightly down on that of the previous year, to 1.84 million tonnes, but would have been higher if some grapes had not been left on the vines because of the then current surplus. The wine regions in eastern Australia had one of their earliest

vintages following good spring rains, unseasonably warm and dry conditions early in the growing season and cool to warm temperatures from spring to harvest. In many regions, vintage was three weeks ahead of normal, the harvest was compressed and finished significantly earlier than usual. Most winemakers had been talking about near-perfect conditions and that it could be an outstanding vintage. The west was less fortunate, with its coolest harvest on record and picking in many places three weeks later than usual. Western Australia's warmer northern areas did best, producing white wines that looked to have come from significantly cooler regions and overall white wines performed much better than reds. The vintage was difficult in Margaret River and more problematic further south.

2005

Not only was the 2005 vintage another record one for the Australian wine industry (with 1.92 million tonnes harvested), but it was one of uniformly super quality. In recent times any increase in the amount harvested has been due to vineyard expansion but in 2005 the increase was due to the ideal weather conditions – a long, mild, growing season and perfectly timed rainfall – which resulted in disease-free fruit and high yields. The exceptions were some parts of the Riverina and eastern Victoria, which were affected by heavy summer rains, and the southern areas of Western Australia, where the late ripening reds suffered because of April rains. Some regions felt that the quality was the best they'd seen in 30 years.

2004

With more than 1.8 million tonnes of grapes harvested, the 2004 vintage was a whopping 25% bigger than 2003's drought-affected crop. There were problems early and late in the season: some of the warmer regions such as the Barossa suffered heat stress (sunburned grapes) in February, and some of the cooler regions such as the Yarra Valley were caught with a few grapes still on the vine when heavy rains hit in April. But between these extremes, quality generally was good to very good. Yields were a little higher than average, too, which eased pressure on the supply of white wines, but only added to the oversupply of reds.

2003

In some ways, a typical Australian vintage – warm and dry – but it was also unusually low-yielding. Indeed, it was the first time for many years that the crop levels were lower than the previous vintage, even with the first harvests from many new vineyards adding to the total. Quality across the board was good to very good, but there were fewer of the superlative wines found in 2002.

2002

Most of south-eastern Australia enjoyed an unusually cool summer, but while this resulted in some of the best grapes ever picked in the large inland regions and warmer premium regions such as the Barossa, the further south in the country you went, the more difficult those cool conditions proved in terms of ripening the grapes. So while 2002 cheap reds often showed the effects of the good vintage – great dark colour, heaps of flavour – and the aromatic whites and chardonnays were certainly unusually flavoursome, you need to be a little choosier buying more expensive wines from the trendier, premium, cooler-climate regions.

For a pleasant daily drop

Try the best cask wines on the market

THE BEST CASK WINES ON THE MARKET

The difficulties experienced by the engine room of the Australian wine industry – along the Murray and Murrumbidgee rivers, in the Riverland, Riverina, Murray–Darling and Swan Hill – in the 2007 vintage relate mainly to substantial reduced crop levels, the lowest in 30 years. At this stage, the price of cask wines has remained stable and there has been a noticeable lift in quality – the result of the lower yields. The average price Australian producers received for exports dropped again last year, from $3.98 per litre to $3.72 per litre, although the volume was up by 8%.

The gentle downhill slide in the popularity of cask wines on the Australian market continues. Well, perhaps that is somewhat of an overstatement. Cask sales continues to represent slightly less than half of the wine sold in Australia – and the amount sold in the past 12 months has dropped by 1.4%, down 2.5 million litres to 179.3 million litres. The amount of fortifieds sold has dropped yet again although the amount of bottled fortified wine is up slightly, so the slump has been in sales of cask fortifieds. As fortified wines are so cheap anyway, it's difficult to complain too much about this.

The volume of white cask wine sold continues to be significantly greater than red wine. Whites make up 66% of table wines sold in casks as against 34% of red wine, whereas the total amount of white wines sold is 58% compared with 42% of red. Cask wine remains the most important segment of the market and the everyday choice of most Australian drinkers.

This is the eighth year in a row that I've tasted all of the cask wines that I've been able to get access to – about a hundred casks per year. There has been a continuation of the improvements that I noted in *Quaff 2006* and *Quaff 2007*, with the best of current red wine casks as good as they've ever been. There is less evidence of chippy oak and dominating added tannins that throw the reds out of balance and leave a powerfully grippy and bitter aftertaste.

The whites too are better than ever. One of the strongest complaints – that cask whites were too sweet – has been addressed. Firstly, well over half of the whites that I received for review were labelled according to the variety or varieties that they contain. Consumers will expect traminer riesling to be sweet and chardonnay to be drier. Secondly, wines labelled 'fresh dry white' were generally drier than casks labelled 'soft fruity white' or 'medium white'. There are, of course, heaps of sweet to very sweet cask whites, but it's easier to spot them that it was and there is more cask white that finishes dry or fairly dry.

All the casks are non-vintage, unless otherwise specified.

> **THE QUAFF 2008 'Platinum Pillow'**
> **CASK WINE OF THE YEAR AWARD**
>
> On the shortlist for this award are:
> **Hardys 'Reserve' Cabernet Sauvignon**
> **Hardys 'Reserve' Shiraz**
> **2006 Yalumba 'Reserve Selection' Rosé Shiraz**
> **2006 Yalumba 'Reserve Selection' Sauvignon Blanc Semillon**
>
> The Yalumba Sauvignon Blanc Semillon is the standout white once again. I love the style of the Yalumba Rosé and it's my sentimental favourite. There's little to choose between the two Hardys reds but I did point the Cabernet higher than the Shiraz and my comments were similarly more enthusiastic. The quality of the Hardys 'Reserve' Cabernet Sauvignon makes it the *Quaff 2008* Cask Wine of the Year.

The reliables – consistent-quality wines, year in, year out

Yalumba is once again the most consistent producer of cask wines – as it has been for all eight editions of *Quaff*. Its whites and rose are better than its reds, with the notable exception of the cask Merlot. Hardys is stronger this year than before and a serious challenger to Yalumba, especially in the red wine sector. De Bortoli was stronger last year than this, but is still a seriously good producer of casks.

Buying and Drinking Casks – Some Tips

Helpful labelling

On all casks you buy, you'll find a date indicating 'best before' or 'packaged on' (the latter mainly on fortifieds). Obviously, the wine will be at its freshest when it is at its youngest – in the first three to six months or so after it is packaged. It will tend to get stale at about nine months, although fortifieds may well last longer.

Towards more meaningful names

There have been dramatic changes in all aspects of the cask wine market, including the names by which the wines are sold. There continues to be an increase in varietal labelling (chardonnay, shiraz ...) and the almost complete disappearance of generic labelling. While I favour varietal labelling over the use of more generalised names ('fresh dry white', 'soft fruity white'), the latter seem to more accurately suggest their contents than they did a few years ago. At least with the examples recommended here, you can expect 'fresh dry white' to be dry.

My grump about the labelling of casks is the continued use of pretentious terms such as 'premium varietal', 'premium', 'cellar choice', 'reserve' and 'reserve selection'. Who do the wine companies (or the marketers) think they are fooling? Do they believe that consumers will be lured into buying a particular cask because they believe that the wine company has kept this exceptional 500 000 litre parcel aside for the Chairman's buddies – and them? Let's get rid of the gobbledegook! Call it 'Renmano 4-litre Chardonnay', 'Yalumba 2-litre Sauvignon Blanc' ... Don't be stupid, keep it simple.

White Casks

 BLOODY GOOD

Hardys 'Reserve' Chardonnay (3 litre) $21

This is just what you want in a cask white: it's clean, fresh and lively with a soft, pleasant mouthfeel, has some ripe peachy varietal character and a zesty dry finish.

2006 Yalumba 'Reserve Selection' Sauvignon Blanc Semillon (2 litre) $13.95

Wow! My tasting notes are identical to what I wrote at this time last year for exactly the same wine – and I had no idea that Yalumba still had stocks of it and were able to enter it again. It says a great deal about the technical expertise of the team at Yalumba that they have this looking in such good condition after a year in tank. The two samples that I had, a year apart, were from different batches – last year's was dated 'Best before Feb 2007' and this year's 'Best before Dec 2007'. Last year, it was the best of the cask whites and runner-up to the Yalumba Merlot for the title of Cask Wine of the Year. This year, it's clearly the best of the cask whites. I'd say again 'This is impressive: fragrant, fresh, lively, deliciously fruity with crisp dry acidity and a lovely fruity finish.' Perhaps I'd be tempted to upgrade the 'lively' to 'vibrant'. The great thing about this wine is that it's fruity yet dry. You won't find a better cask white.

 GOOD

Banrock Station Chardonnay (2 litre) $13.50

This is a well-made Riverland chardonnay that is fresh, clean and lively with attractive, ripe fruity flavours and a gentle easy drinking finish. It's uncomplicated but pleasant.

WHITE CASKS

De Bortoli 'Premium' Traminer Riesling (4 litre) $18.95

This would be my pick of the sweeter cask whites: an attractive fruity wine with fragrant gewürztraminer aromas that are spicy and grapey. Those flavours are present, too, on the palate. It's very pleasant drinking and is filled out by a sweetness that is not excessive.

Lindemans 'Cellar Choice' Soft Fruity White (4 litre) $11.95

This is for those who prefer their cask whites a little bit sweeter than me. It's well made with spicy, grapey fruit flavours, is clean, fresh and sweet but not cloying on the finish. I'm impressed by the smart new livery from Lindemans, which makes the cask seem more compact than before.

Renmano 'Premium Varietal' Semillon Sauvignon Blanc Chardonnay (4 litre) $17.50

Few would be disappointed with this – it's clean, fresh and fruit: bright and lively, too.

Sunnyvale Dry White (4 litre) $10

This is by far the best of the Sunnyvale whites and terrific value at the price: clean, fresh and delightfully fruity with a good mouthfeel and a dry finish. Just what they promised.

2006 Yalumba Riesling (2 litre) $13.95

Another excellent-value cask from Yalumba. It's lively, fresh and spotlessly clean, brightly fruity and pleasant to drink with a crisp, dry finish that lingers.

◗ PRETTY GOOD

Banrock Station Semillon Chardonnay (2 litre) $13.50

This looked fresher, cleaner, livelier than the wines which surrounded it in the *Quaff* tastings. It's pretty restrained yet pleasantly dry.

CASK WINES

Cross Country Crisp Dry White (4 litre) $7.95

> The best of the casks from the Riverina producer, Beelgara (formerly Rosetto). It has a pleasant fruity lift, decent straightforward flavours and a reasonably dry finish. Amazingly cheap.

De Bortoli Semillon Sauvignon Blanc (2 litre) $13.95

> This is well made and pleasant, if a bit bland, but with a decent dryish finish.

Golden Gate Medium Dry White (4 litre) $10

> As the name 'medium dry' suggests, this is pretty sweet. It's a decent cask white that is clean, fresh and fruity with a sweetness that is not excessive.

Lachlan Ridge Semillon Sauvignon Blanc (2 litre) $9

> This is fresh, clean and lively with decent flavour and a pleasant dry finish of good length. Exclusive to Vintage Cellars.

Lindemans 'Cellar Choice' Crisp Dry White (4 litre) $11.95

> Much better than last year's wine, this is clean, fresh and lively with fruity flavours and an attractive dry finish.

2006 Long Flat Semillon Sauvignon Blanc (1 litre) $9.90

> I like the idea of the 1-litre cask and I imagine that it'll find a slot in the market. This is clean, well made and pleasantly dry.

Morris 'Premium' Dry White (4 litre) $18.95

> What you see is what you get. This is clean, fresh and pleasantly fruity with a decent dry finish.

Tangled Vine Fresh Dry White (4 litre) $8

> This is the first year that I've seen Vintage Cellars enter the cask wine market. The wine is well made and is fresh and clean with fruity flavours. However, it's a bit sweeter than you'd expect. Exclusive to Vintage Cellars.

WHITE CASKS

Tangled Vine Soft Fruity White (4 litre) $8
>This is fresh and fruity with some grapey flavours and a sweet (though not too sweet) finish. Exclusive to Vintage Cellars.

2006 Yalumba Chardonnay (2 litre) $13.95
>The Yalumba stamp can be relied on. This is clean, fresh and lively with pleasing fruity flavours and a dry finish.

Yalumba Classic Dry White (2 litre) $11.95
>A pleasant, well-made white that is clean, fresh and easy drinking.

Yalumba Spatlese Fruity White (2 litre) $11.95
>This has some fragrance, is clean, fresh and sweet – yet not too sweet.

Pink Casks

🍾 BLOODY GOOD

2006 Yalumba 'Reserve Selection' Rosé Shiraz (2 litre) $13.95

This is terrific. There's heaps of strawberry and musk stick aromas, a soft round and juicy palate, admirably intense, bright strawberry and red cherry flavours and a pleasing dryish finish. On the website I reported on the first of the Yalumba cask rosés, which my records indicate was a non-vintage blend. I received an email from Brian Walsh of Yalumba explaining that he had been disappointed that it wasn't ready for last year's *Quaff* and that he thought it 'bloody terrific'. Brian continued that he 'took one home off the bottling line last week, as I often do, to watch the progress of this important part of our portfolio and Margot said how great it would be in a jug with ice (and possibly other "condiments") as a refreshing summer drink and I couldn't agree more'. The 2006 has greater fruit intensity and more vibrancy. I think it's as good as a cask wine gets.

🍾 PRETTY GOOD

Kaiser Stuhl Rosé (5 litre) $12.95

The sweetness here makes the texture silky-smooth, the flavours are restrained yet attractive and the sweetness on the finish is balanced by acidity. The price will please many.

Red Casks

🍾 BLOODY GOOD

⭐ Hardys 'Reserve' Cabernet Sauvignon (3 litre) $21

THE QUAFF 2008 'Platinum Pillow'
CASK WINE OF THE YEAR AWARD

This is a very impressive cask wine: indeed, it's a surprise packet. There's heaps of bright, ripe red cherry and redcurrant flavours, soft, round, almost lush texture, so smooth and approachable drinking.

Hardys 'Reserve' Shiraz (3 litre) $21

The team at Hardys have had a great year making cask wines in the Riverland. What a brilliant pair this makes with the Hardys Cabernet cask. It's the more restrained of the two on the nose and shows juicy dark berry flavours, some succulence, restrained oak and tannins and an attractive lingering finish.

2006 Yalumba 'Reserve Selection' Merlot (2 litre) $13.95

This was last year's winner of the Platinum Pillow, for best cask wine. It was a non-vintage blend (labelled 'best before February 2007): this is a vintage wine (labelled 'best before March 2008'). The style is remarkably similar to the previous one: vibrant, supple, round and easy drinking, packed with ripe redcurrant and dark plum flavours and gently grippy tannins. Perfect with rare roast beef and certainly improved by being served with food.

🍾 GOOD

De Bortoli 'Premium Reserve' Shiraz (2 litre) $13.95

Last year, I preferred the De Bortoli Cabernet cask, but in 2007 I'm more impressed by this delightful Shiraz.

It's aromatically fruity, has lively redcurrant and dark berry flavours, is supple and smooth with some firmness to finish. As you'd expect, it perfectly approachable when consumed with food – perhaps good-quality sausages with mash, fried onions and a healthy salad.

2006 Yalumba 'Reserve Selection' Cabernet Merlot
(2 litre) $13.95

There's a pleasing lightness about this bright, fruity red – heaps of ripe redcurrant, red plum flavours and a gentle finish that lingers.

 **GOOD**

Banrock Station Cabernet Merlot (2 litre) $13.50

Dark berry flavours, restrained oak and tannins, firm to finish but OK with a hearty stew.

De Bortoli 'Premium Reserve' Merlot (2 litre) $13.95

There's a pleasing dryness about this cask red: clean, fresh, dark berry flavours with restrained oak and tannins.

Lachlan Ridge Shiraz Cabernet (2 litre) $9

This is another of the Vintage Cellars labels for cask wine. It's soft and pleasant with gentle red berry flavour and balanced oak and tannins. Exclusive to Vintage Cellars.

Renmano 'Premium Varietal' Shiraz Cabernet Merlot
(4 litre) $21.50

I've complained earlier about the use of pompous names to describe cask wines. It's worse when the marketers don't even describe the wine accurately, as with this wine. As we all know, a varietal wine is one made from a single variety. So we would expect a 'premium varietal' to be a distinguished wine from a single variety, not a blend of three varieties. By the way, the wine is decent: light red berry flavours, supple and quite smooth with a gentle grip to finish.

Sunnyvale Medium Dry Red (4 litre) $10

There appears to be an improvement in quality with this Sunnyvale range. This is cleaner and fresher than many of the cheaper casks; there's red berry flavours, too sweet for me but the sweetness is balanced by cleansing acidity. Many will like it.

Yalumba Classic Dry Red (2 litre) $11.95

This is soft, round and fruity with restrained tannins and a dryish finish.

2006 Yalumba 'Reserve Selection' Cabernet Sauvignon (2 litre) $13.95

I've consistently preferred the Yalumba Merlot cask to this and the Yalumba Shiraz cask. I can't help thinking these should be better. There is plenty of fruit flavour but I find this tight and firm and less easy drinking than the Merlot.

2006 Yalumba 'Reserve Selection' Shiraz (2 litre) $13.95

Better on the palate than on the nose, supple quite fleshy texture, dark berry flavours and a reasonably firm finish.

Fortified Casks

🍾 BLOODY GOOD

Stanley Premium Tawny (2 litre) $9.95

Pick of the tawny bunch: restrained on the nose, silky smooth, almost lush, tight and quite fine, sweet in a restrained way thanks to the cleansing crisp dry acidity.

Seppelt 'Solero' Extra Dry Sherry (2 litre) $14.95

There's a strongish rancio character on the nose, intense salty, sea-spray flavours and a pleasingly dry grip to finish. It's a wine of character in good condition.

🍾 GOOD

Penfolds 'Wood Age' Muscat (2 litre) $14.95

A consistent performer. The current batch is malty on the nose, sweet and gently lush with the flavours of fresh grapes and honey. It's quite lively and bright and lightly framed.

🍾 PRETTY GOOD

De Bortoli 'Premium' Liqueur Muscat (4 litre) $20.95

There's a strong raisiny aroma on the nose and heaps of raisiny flavours. It's lush and sweet, a bit too sweet for me, before a flavourful finish that lingers.

Hardys Tawny (3 litre) $21

There's a hint of rancio and some toffee flavours, sweetness on the mid-palate and plenty of spirit on the finish. It's easy drinking and not over the top.

McWilliam's 'Premium Selection' Tawny (2 litre) $12

> There's a good depth of dark berry fruit flavours, some raisins and prunes, lush texture: it's sweet but not cloying.

Morris Tawny Port (2 litre) $12.95

> Subdued on the nose, showing toffee, treacle and a hint of liquorice and molasses flavours, with pleasing sweetness.

Penfolds 'Wood Aged' Port (2 litre) $14.95

> Still fresh and lively with syrupy toffee flavours and significant sweetness.

Seppelt 'Solero' Sweet Sherry (2 litre) $14.95

> There's malt and toffee flavours, texture that is almost lush, and pronounced sweetness on the mid-palate. It finishes long and sweet yet is not cloying. Will appeal widely.

More than froth and bubble

Sparkling wines under $15

SPARKLING WINES UNDER $15

Hardys has certainly done as well as usual in the sparkling wine arena of *Quaff*. It continues the remarkable feat – unparalleled in the history of the world – of having the Banrock Station Sparkling Pinot Chardonnay and the 'Reserve' Sparkling Shiraz rated 'Bloody Good' in all the eight editions of *Quaff*. I've run out of words to describe it (where do you go after 'hat-trick' and the awful but catchy Americanism 'threepeat') but the Pinot Noir Chardonnay wins Best Sparkling under $10 for the fourth year in a row; and the Banrock Station 'Reserve' Sparkling Shiraz – Wine of the Year in 2005 – is the highest ranked sparkling red once again.

Quaff's Sparkling Wine of the Year for the past two years – Hardys' Sir James Pinot Noir Chardonnay – has risen in price (as have all the Hardys bubblies, though they are still bargains) so it is ineligible for an award here. It's still in great shape, though, and heartily recommended once again. I'll bet it's readily available for less than $15 in many wine stores.

Having said that, the Yellowglen range has been reliably good in recent years and is getting better. I'm impressed with the consistency of the Yellowglen sparkling range, from the 2005 Yellowglen Pinot Noir Chardonnay to 'Yellow', 'Pink', 'Red' and 'Bella'. The introduction of the low-alcohol (and low-calorie) 'Jewel

Yellow' and 'Jewel Pink' has been well handled and they are screamingly good (especially 'Jewel Yellow').

I have a major problem with the marketing of budget-priced sparkling wines, in particular with the way companies use French words associated with champagne as part of their names. In my view, the use of words like 'brut' (which means 'dry' in French) and 'cuvée' (a blend) are pointless, even silly. What consumer is going to be impressed by adding 'Brut', 'Brut de Brut', 'Brut Cuvée' or 'Grande Cuvée' to the name of a bubbly? What will most customers make of the difference between the Seaview Brut and the Seaview Brut de Brut? Just as ludicrous is the use of the term 'Reserve' to describe these large-volume sparkling wines – especially when there is no standard wine.

Thank goodness for straightforward, no-nonsense marketing and names such as Omni Non-Vintage, Omni 'Blue', McGuigan 'Black Label' Sparkling Chardonnay, Yellowglen 'Yellow' and Banrock Station Pinot Noir Chardonnay.

All sparkling wines are non-vintage, unless otherwise indicated.

SPARKLING WINES UNDER $15

THE QUAFF 2008 'You Can Launch My Ship'
SPARKLING WINE OF THE YEAR AWARD

On the shortlist for this award are:
Banrock Station Pinot Chardonnay
Banrock Station 'Reserve' Sparkling Shiraz
2007 Brown Brothers 'Zibibbo'
Yellowglen 'Jewel Yellow'

The qualities of the Banrock Station wines and their track records speak for themselves. Yellowglen 'Jewel' is an innovative marketing concept that has been pulled off with a bloody good bubbly in the case of the 'Jewel Yellow'. I love 'Zibibbo' – great name – which is a clever and natural development from the success that Brown Brothers have had with their moscato and is a delicious sweet bubbly, still with low alcohol. It's the *Quaff 2008* Sparkling Wine of the Year.

THE QUAFF 2008 'Baubles, Bubbles and Beads'
BEST SPARKLING UNDER $10 AWARD

On the shortlist for this award are:
Angus Brut
Banrock Station Sparkling Pinot Noir Chardonnay
Michinbury White Seal

It's remarkable that three of the six 'Bloody Goods' in the Sparkling White section are under $10. Amazing that our winemakers can produce such terrific bubblies at those prices. The Minchinbury White Seal shone when other representatives of this once great budget-priced label are not as consistently good as they once were: its creamy texture and zesty acidity are so refreshing. The Angas Brut is even better than it was last year. It's fresh and clean and pure with some authentic sparkling wine characters. But I am giving the award once again to the Banrock Station. It shone in the tasting as the definitive style with light, freshy, bubbly character, creaminess and a gentle easy-drinking finish, albeit with a touch of sweetness. It's the *Quaff 2008* Best Sparkling under $10.

The reliables – consistent-quality wines, year in, year out

Banrock Station Pinot Chardonnay and Banrock Station Reserve Sparkling Shiraz (2004 Wine of the Year) have appeared in each edition of *Quaff*. The Brown Brothers Moscato (2002 Wine of the Year) has appeared in seven of the eight editions of *Quaff*.

Buying and Drinking Bubbly – Some Tips

Look for places with a quick turnover

The most impressive wines have clean, fresh, lively, up-front flavours. As these wines don't improve with cellaring, buy from shops that have a quick turnover of stock.

Drink cold

These budget-priced quaffers are best served nicely chilled to enhance their fresh, lively character and zingy acidity. Enjoy and quaff on!

Corked?

The advent of screwcaps as a closure of choice for much of the Australian and New Zealand wine industry has changed my life as a wine taster because I see significantly fewer corked wines now. This is especially so with the tastings for *Quaff* where the majority of bottles I am sent are sealed with screwcaps. However, most sparkling wines still use cork as a closure – the exceptions are Domaine Chandon and Seppelt Great Western (with their expensive wines). As a result, I've seen more corked wines in the *Quaff* sparkling wine tastings compared to other tastings. My suggestion is that when you are trying sparkling wines you swirl, sniff and check that there are no strange off characters before you drink. Look for any mouldy, wet-hessian, wet-dog aromas: anything that doesn't seem quite right. If you're not sure ask.

– SPARKLING WINES UNDER $15

White Sparkling

🍾 BLOODY GOOD

Angas Brut $7.95

This is up a notch from last year with a remarkably similar tasting note. It's fresh and clean, soft and round, with delightfully creamy texture, pristine citrus and bready yeast flavours before a gentle, fine finish that lingers. A quintessential quaffing bubbly.

⭐ Banrock Station Sparkling Pinot Noir Chardonnay $7.95

THE QUAFF 2008 'Baubles, Bubbles and Beads'
BEST SPARKLING UNDER $10 AWARD

The most consistent budget-priced bubbly of the past six years, the Banrock Station bubbly remains impressive. There was a slight whiff of confectionery on the nose when it was first opened but that blew off. Other than that it's very much in the style we've come to expect: fresh, clean and lively, soft and round in the middle palate, light and fine with creamy texture before a gentle easy-drinking finish with some noticeable sweetness.

Minchinbury 'White Seal' $6.95

Like the Angas Brut, this was rated at Good last year and is lifted to the higher rating with a pleasingly similar review: it is light-bodied, clean and lively with creamy texture, good balance, finesse and fresh, zippy acidity.

Sir James Non-Vintage $16.50

This has been the Sparkling Wine of the Year for the past two years, so the price has drifted up by almost $2. I've included it in this chapter (although it will not be eligible for any awards) as I'm confident it will be available on discount and it's as good as ever. Soft, round and wonderful current drinking, with seductive yeasty flavours, creamy texture and gentle fresh acidity.

Yellowglen 'Jewel Yellow' $13.95

This is the low-alcohol version of 'Yellow' and, to my surprise, I marginally preferred it to its sibling. This has bready, yeasty, lemony citrus characters, is tight and fine, with good intensity and power, rich creamy texture and balanced crisp acidity. With its 6% alcohol by volume, it's being promoted as having 30% fewer calories than the standard 'Yellow'.

Yellowglen 'Yellow' $13.95

I think it's a matter of style and personal preference whether you prefer this or the low-alcohol version. 'Yellow' is bolder, more powerful, with cool appley flavours, a steely core and strong firm acidity. You choose.

 **GOOD**

Coldstone Brut $12

This is a label from the Victorian Alps winery which shows intensity and finesse with its yeasty characters, a tight almost steely structure and powerful, no-holds-barred acidity.

Killawarra Brut $9.95

This is fresh, clean and lively – even vibrant – with power and finesse, heaps of bold yeasty characters and refreshing zippy acidity.

Matthew Lang Brut Cuvée $5.95

This label springs another surprise. The bubbly is clean, fresh and lively with creamy texture, some fruitiness, a hint of yeast and bright, crisp acidity that produces a dry finish. All that for $5.95. I am surprised.

SPARKLING WINES UNDER $15

Nepenthe 'Tryst' Pinot Noir Chardonnay $16.90

A first for this Adelaide Hills producer under their budget label, Tryst, so expect to see it discounted below $15, especially now they are owned by McGuigan Simeon. It's a restrained style that is soft and round with some yeast character – all too easy to drink.

Pirramimma 'Pirra' Sparkling Chardonnay $17

I love a wine that is what it says it is. No nonsensical 'bruts' and 'cuvées' and 'special reserves': it says it's 'Sparkling Chardonnay' and it is! Picking the grapes early and using them as a sparkling base is a good way to use the McLaren Vale's nondescript chardonnay. This is uncomplicated, unpretentious and very attractive drinking: fresh, clean and lively with lemon citrus characters, softened by some sweetness on the finish, but with zesty acidity to cleanse the palate.

Taltarni 'T Series' Chardonnay Pinot Noir Pinot Meunier $14.95

Taltarni has made some excellent sparkling wines over the years and this is a first under the newish budget range. It is crisp and bold with intense lemon citrus, apple and yeast flavours, a tight structure, finesse and zippy acidity.

Tulloch Cuvée Brut $13

A delightful Hunter Valley bubbly for a fair price. It's clean, fresh and intense with an attractive creamy texture and zesty gentle acidity that lingers.

2005 Yellowglen Pinot Noir Chardonnay $16.95

This is a bubbly that would be terrific with food, in fact it needs food to tone it down: bold yeasty flavours, creamy texture, and a rich, powerful and zesty to finish.

WHITE SPARKLING

🍾 PRETTY GOOD

Cockatoo Ridge Brut Cuvée $9.95

This is very much in the Cockatoo Ridge style so it's big, bold and powerful with a tight structure, intensity of flavour and grippy acidity. I preferred last year's blend but if you like this kind of sparkling wine – and plenty do – the price is right.

Deakin Estate Brut $14.95

From Red Cliffs in the Murray–Darling comes this well made yet uncomplicated sparkling white that is restrained, clean and fresh with pleasant lemon citrus flavour.

Jacob's Creek Chardonnay Pinot Noir $13.95

There's some candied confectionery character on the nose and a bold powerful zesty palate.

Jean Pierre Brut $5

The best of this year's wines from Jean Pierre & Co, which I've described as 'decent fizz'. It doesn't have great character but is clean and lively with gentle fresh acidity.

McWilliam's 'Hanwood' Pinot Noir Chardonnay $12

There's attractive yeastiness on the nose, while this bubbly is fresh, clean and lively with creamy texture and a gentle finish. It's an uncomplicated bubbly at a fair price.

Minchinbury Brut $6.95

Here is a clean, fresh, even zippy young bubbly that shows some citrus and lemon citrus flavours. Good value at this price.

Orlando 'Trilogy' Pinot Noir Chardonnay Pinot Meunier $15.95

Another old favourite up in price but expect to find it below $15 on special. It has some floral aromas, is light, fresh and lively, with appley flavours and a pleasantly gentle finish.

Preece Sparkling $14

There's a touch of musk stick confectionery on the nose: it's clean, fresh and has good intensity.

Queen Adelaide Brut $7.95

While there's not a great deal of flavour, it is clean, fresh and easy to drink, thanks to its gentle creamy acidity.

Yalumba 'Dunes' Pinot Noir Chardonnay $14.95

A pleasant, easy-drinking bubbly that is well made and finishes with refreshing crisp acidity.

Pink Sparkling

▄▄▶ GOOD

Omni 'Pink' $12.50
This is up in price and appears sweeter than last year's version, but is still a terrific sparkling wine. It's vibrant pink with raspberry and strawberry flavours, soft, creamy texture with an attractive hint of sweetness to finish.

▄▄▶ PRETTY GOOD

Banrock Station Sparkling White Shiraz $9.50
This is soft and sweet with pleasing strawberries and cream characters, is filled out in the mid-palate by its sweetness before a gentle finish.

Cockatoo Ridge Sparkling Rosé $9.95
While not quite up to the quality of last year's wine, this is clean, fresh and light with yeasty, strawberry notes and a gentle, slightly sweet finish.

Yellowglen 'Jewel Pink' $13.95
This has attractive strawberry characters on the nose and palate, some sweetness, and finishes clean and crisp. It is lower in alcohol (and therefore calories) than the Yellowglen 'Pink' and is much softer and less boldly acidic.

Red Sparkling

🍾 BLOODY GOOD

Banrock Station 'Reserve' Sparkling Shiraz $12.49

This continues its remarkable run at the top of our sparkling red division. With the Penfolds Reserve Club Aged Tawny, it has had the longest run at the top of any wine section in *Quaff*. I love the wine and believe it's definitely good enough to drink with the Christmas goose (turkey or duck) and irresistible enough to quaff at pretty well any other time. It's good as an aperitif or at the end of the meal with plum pudding, or sticky date pudding, or New Norcia Nut Cake. This year I commented on its heady aromatics, rich, concentrated and powerful brambly, mulberry and blackcurrant flavours, mid-palate sweetness, and noted that it was impeccably balanced by moderate, ripe tannins.

Bleasdale Sparkling Shiraz $17.50

The Potts family have been making wine at Bleasdale in Langhorne Creek for more than 150 years and make some excellent wines, especially the reds. This is fabulous: rich, concentrated, dense and deep vanilla bean, brambly, dark wild-forest berry flavours, creamy texture and balanced finish that lingers.

🍾 GOOD

Wyndham Estate 'Bin 555' Sparkling Shiraz $13.95

A consistent style given the same ranking as last year, with identical tasting notes and scores. Still that wonderfully fleshy, velvety texture, depth of blackberry, black cherry, dark plum flavours and clean, refreshing finish.

RED SPARKLING

🍾 PRETTY GOOD

Black Chook Sparkling Shiraz $17.95

It's the guys from Woop Woop – the wine label, not the town – Ben Riggs and Tony Parkinson from Pennys Hill. The wine has a following among those who like their sparkling reds rich and deeply concentrated, robust, powerful and tannic. Not for the faint of heart.

2004 Leasingham 'Magnus' Sparkling Shiraz $14.95

A new range for this Clare Valley producer, which has a formidable reputation for sparkling reds – some of the best and most ageworthy produced in the country. This is soft, round, creamily textured with vanilla bean and plum jam characters and sweetness balanced by tannins and acidity.

Omni 'Red' $12.50

A straightforward style that is soft, round and very easy drinking, with ripe plummy flavours and noticeable sweetness.

Yellowglen 'Red' $13.95

This is softer, rounder, less oaky and less robust than last year's wine, with ripe plummy flavours, still that creamy texture and perceptible sweetness to finish.

SPARKLING WINES UNDER $15

Sweet Sparkling

🍾 BLOODY GOOD

2007 Innocent Bystander Moscato (375 ml) $13.50

I think this is fabulous! The packaging of 375 ml bottles with crown seal and the tinge of pink in the wine set up the expectation. And the lightly bubbly, gently fragrant sweet fizz delivers Australia's premier moscato. It's vibrant, pristine, sweet and grapey, surprisingly fine, and finishes with bright cleansing acidity. Delicious.

2007 Two Hands 'Brilliant Disguise' Moscato $18

Fabulous example of this sweet fizzy white from the Barossa-based Two Hands winery. It's delightfully fragrant and floral with intense grapey, rose petal flavours, fine, delicate and fruity finishing with impeccably balanced refreshing and cleansing crisp acidity.

⭐ **2007 Brown Brothers 'Zibibbo'** $14.95

THE QUAFF 2008 'You Can Launch My Ship'
SPARKLING WINE OF THE YEAR AWARD

This is a delicious new wine from the Brown family – no doubt sparking off the success of their moscato – in this case with a fully sparkling wine rather than the spritzy, lightly fizzy moscato. They've kept the alcohol low – at 6% – and used the Italian word for muscat as the name. It has excellent intensity of sweet grapey flavours and very impressive fresh, almost bracing, acidity which cleanses the palate.

Omni 'Blue' $9.95

Since its introduction a couple of years ago, this has been a consistent delight: lively, even vibrant moscato style, sweet but with racy acidity that cuts though that sweetness and leaves you ready for another drink.

SWEET SPARKLING

Nova Moscato $9.95

> The guys at the Riverina's Westend have been working on this moscato and I must say that I think this is a cracker. With moscato's characteristic low alcohol (in this case 9% alcohol by volume) you can drink much more without worry about being over the limit. There's grapey aromas, intense rose petal, lychee and grape flavours, a soft round and sweet mid-palate that is tamed by refreshing crisp acidity. Value.

▭ GOOD

2007 Brown Brothers Moscato $15.90

> One of the Reliables, still present after all these years. This is clean, fresh and vibrant, with its sweetness tamed by racy acidity on the finish.

2006 Brown Brothers Moscato $15.95

> This is similarly attractive but too sweet for me. I'd prefer it with livelier crisper acidity.

De Bortoli 'Vittorio' Spumante $5

> A well-made lightly fizzy drink that has lively sweet grapey flavours and a vibrant sweet finish. Cheap as chips: well, perhaps cheaper.

2007 Long Flat Moscato $9.90

> From the Cheviot Bridge team comes this wonderfully aromatic moscato with rose petal, lychee and grape flavours that is super sweet. Too sweet for me but very good value for those who like the sweetness.

Omni 'Citrus' $9.95

> This is not a bubbly that I'd drink but it's well made and will appeal. There's strong lemon and lime citrus flavours and plenty of sweetness but this is admirably balanced by cleansing acidity.

SPARKLING WINES UNDER $15

2006 Trentham Estate 'La Famiglia' Moscato $12.50

> A terrific moscato from the Murray–Darling that is in the style – low in alcohol, clean, fresh, grapey and sweet with crisp acidity.

🍾 PRETTY GOOD

Chalk Hill Moscato $14.95

> From a small McLaren Vale label with three vineyards in the region comes this pleasantly grapey, sweet moscato cleaned up by some lively acidity.

Yellowglen 'Bella' $16.95

> A sweet grapey bubbly in the moscato style, clean, fresh and well made except that it's too sweet. If that's the way you want it, this could well be for you.

Bottled sunshine

White wines under $15

WHITE WINES UNDER $15

THE QUAFF 2008 'Whooshable'
WHITE WINE OF THE YEAR AWARD

On the shortlist for this award are:
2006 Angove's 'Nine Vines' Viognier
2007 Jim Barry Watervale Riesling
2007 Ferngrove 'Symbols' Sauvignon Blanc Semillon
2007 Peter Lehmann Eden Valley Riesling
2007 Primo Estate 'La Biondina' Colombard Sauvignon Blanc
2007 Sandalford 'Element' Classic White

Both Rieslings show excellent regional character (Clare in the case of the Jim Barry and Eden Valley with the Peter Lehmann), intensity of flavour, and are classy ageworthy whites. The Angove's Viognier shows the affinity that the variety can have for our warm regions and has a poise that I find most attractive. The Ferngrove Sauvignon Blanc Semillon has a fresh vibrance and purity of flavour that is most appealing, while 'La Biondina' dances on the tongue as always with a refreshing zestiness that almost talks of summer. The 'Element' Classic White transforms an excellent vintage in the underrated Swan Valley by playing to the region's strengths – chenin blanc and verdelho – and illustrates how delightful quaffing wine can be.

The point of all this, is that any one of the shortlisted wines would be worthy winners. I've chosen the 2007 Peter Lehmann Eden Valley Riesling, mainly because of the impact it has had on me when I've tasted it. It is so delightfully fragrant, so pure and fine, and so mouthwateringly delicious that any attempts to resist are likely to fail. Quaff on!

THE QUAFF 2008 'The Gluggable'
BEST WHITE WINE UNDER $10 AWARD

On the shortlist for this award are:
2006 Angove's 'Long Row' Chardonnay
2007 De Bortoli 'Montage' Semillon Sauvignon Blanc
2006 Leasingham 'Circa 1893' Chardonnay
2006 Leasingham 'Circa 1893' Riesling

What an auspicious debut the 'Circa 1893' label has made for the Clare Valley's Leasingham and what a pretty useful way to introduce Simon Osicka to the Chief Winemaker's role there. The Chardonnay is a delightful quaffer while the Riesling is a notch up – still delightfully drinkable but poised and focused in a way that budget-priced wines rarely are. De Bortoli took this trophy last year with their 'Sacred Hill' Colombard Chardonnay and have come close with their 'Montage' Semillon Sauvignon Blanc, which has as much flavour as you can pack into such a well-priced white.

However, I've awarded the 2006 Angove's 'Long Row' Chardonnay as the Best White Wine under $10 because it's made in a style that is so different from most chardonnays at this price point. It packs intense white peach flavours with complexity and finesse, and an almost savoury drinkability.

CHARDONNAY

I don't hear much from the ABC (Anything But Chardonnay) group or those who bleat that they find chardonnay boring. The reality is that chardonnay is by far the most widely planted white wine grape in Australia – making up 44.2% of all the white winegrape vineyard area planted in Australia (31 200 hectares). Plantings in the past two years have slowed down, but last year more chardonnay (737 hectares) was planted than any other variety, white or red.

The amount of chardonnay harvested was over 423 000 tonnes (in 2006), close to double its production three years earlier. Its closest white grape rivals are semillon (96 500 tonnes), colombard (80 000 tonnes – down 9000 tonnes on the previous year), muscat gordo blanco (56 000 tonnes) and riesling (42 000 tonnes). Shiraz maintains its position as Australia's most popular grape although chardonnay is closing the gap and is well ahead of cabernet sauvignon.

The great strength of the Australian wine industry is its technological expertise and, in particular, its ability to produce large volumes of good to very good quality wine at reasonable prices. As a result, relatively few of the wines I have tasted for *Quaff* show winemaking faults. Many of those not reviewed lack concentration of flavour, and appear bland and dull. This may have occurred as a result of overcropping in the vineyard or sourcing the wines from very young vines. Even in the last couple of vintages, there has been a significant reduction in the number of chardonnays that are too heavily oaked or show oak characters that are very charry or chippy. Clumsy winemaking, however, does mean that some whites have too much residual sugar and so appeared overly sweet.

Many Australian chardonnays have a ripe fruit sweetness that is a large part of their popularity. There is a great difference between this fruit sweetness and sugar sweetness. Many chardonnays under $15 are softened and rounded out by a touch of residual sugar. Too much, however, spoils the balance of the wine and makes it taste syrupy or overly sweet on the finish.

Chardonnays that sell at $10 or below need to be sourced wholly, or in large part, from the warm to hot irrigated areas along the Murray in South Australia, Victoria or New South Wales and on the Murrumbidgee in the Riverina. The best tend to be delicious, straightforward whites which rely on ripe fruit flavours for their easy drinkability. With careful viticulture and meticulous winemaking, it is possible to produce some of these wines in huge volumes without risking quality or consistency.

Chardonnays that sell for more than $10 are sourced, at least in part, from premium wine regions and from lower yielding vineyards. With more concentrated fruit, it is possible to use winemaking techniques that will produce more complex and therefore more interesting wines. These will be more full-bodied, have more weight, more richness, greater concentration and power.

The reliables – consistent-quality wines, year in, year out

Regular recommendations over the eight editions of *Quaff* include McWilliam's 'Hanwood' and Rosemount Estate 'Diamond Label'. The price of the latter has crept up a bit though I suspect it would almost always be sold for less than $15.

Buying and Drinking Chardonnay – Some Tips

Can real chardonnay be unoaked?

There are certainly some who believe that without oak chardonnay is dull and bland or, at least, incapable of realising its potential. While I do think that clever or careful use of quality oak lifts chardonnay to new heights, there are always some excellent unwooded chardonnays reviewed in *Quaff*. At least those rated as 'Bloody Good' are fresh, clean and wonderfully youthful and – in quality terms – the equal of any (or almost any) of the wines in this chapter.

Zesty youth

One important difference between oaked and unoaked chardonnay is that the latter do rely on the first flush of youth for their vibrance and so are best within two years of vintage. Oaked chardonnay can be aged for a little bit longer. Having said that, most of the wines reviewed here are best drunk in the next 12 months – when their ripe fruit flavours are at their freshest and most exuberant.

Unwooded Chardonnay

🍾 BLOODY GOOD

2006 Xanadu 'Dragon' Unwooded Chardonnay $16

Here's an indication of the Xanadu revival of this Margaret River winery under the Rathbone family – along with a gold medal at one of the wine shows for the 2006 Chardonnay which I loved. It's clean, fresh and vibrant with intense melon and ripe tropical flavours, a good mouthfeel and a bracing finish. Uncomplicated and delicious.

🍾 GOOD

2006 Willow Bridge Unwooded Chardonnay $15.50
2007 Willow Bridge Unwooded Chardonnay $15.50

The largest producer in the beautiful Ferguson Valley (in the Geographe region) makes superb aromatic whites. The 2007 is lightly aromatic with fresh pure passionfruit flavours and a zippy finish that lingers. The 2006 is also likely to be on the shelves: it's just about as good (maybe the 2007 is more vibrant) and my tasting notes are similar.

2006 Wirra Wirra 'Scrubby Rise' Unwooded Chardonnay $14.95

This is soft, round and very easy to drink, with gentle fruitiness and clean, refreshing, crisp acidity to finish.

🍾 PRETTY GOOD

2006 Alkoomi Unwooded Chardonnay $13.50

This is a decent drink, a touch lacking in concentration, but cool and pleasant in the mouth.

WHITE WINES UNDER $15

2005 Growers 'Peppermint Grove' Unwooded Chardonnay $13.95

From the Margaret River-based group, here is a soft, round, easy-drinking chardonnay that has good varietal character and is fully ripe with balanced acidity.

2006 Oakway Unwooded Chardonnay $14

This new vineyard, at Donnybrook in the Geographe region, has produced a straightforward (ironically) unoaked chardonnay that is fresh, clean and pleasant to drink.

2006 Preston Vale Unwooded Chardonnay $9.90

This is from an investment vineyard in Geographe and is an uncomplicated drink. It has reasonable varietal character and is clean and fresh, but lacks depth or concentration of flavour.

2006 Watershed 'Shades' Unwooded Chardonnay $16.95

This chardonnay from the south of Margaret River has clean, fresh sweet tropical fruit flavours.

Chardonnay

🍾 BLOODY GOOD

⭐ 2006 Angove's 'Long Row' Chardonnay $9.95
THE QUAFF 2008 'The Gluggable'
BEST WHITE WINE UNDER $10 AWARD

In the past 18 months or so, the Angove's team has been making some of the best budget-priced wines in the country. This is different from the ripe, plump 'sunshine in a bottle' wines that made our chardonnays popular worldwide. It much more elegant, tighter and finer than those: with intense, white peach flavours, a pleasing mouthfeel and gentle soft finish.

2006 De Bortoli 'Windy Peak' Chardonnay $14.95

Windy Peak is a Victorian label for De Bortoli and is produced at their Dixons Creek winery in the Yarra. This has attractive stone-fruit flavours, reasonable weight, lively acidity which highlights some lingering peachiness on the finish.

2006 Devil's Lair 'Fifth Leg' Chardonnay $18.95

When this is available under $15 – and I suspect that it'll be most of the time – it's a bargain. The first vintage of a chardonnay under the Devil's Lair second label is a resounding success. It is fragrant, has ripe peach, pineapple and other tropical delights, creamy fleshy texture as well as balance and elegance. Fantastic flavour.

2006 Gnangara Chardonnay $12

This budget-priced label has benefited from the chardonnay program of the now defunct Evans & Tate. Clever winemaking has produced a terrific Western Australian chardonnay that has ripe peachy flavours, an appealing mouthfeel and delicious quaffability.

2006 Grant Burge 'Barossa Vines' Chardonnay $14.75

I think of the Barossa as Australia's greatest shiraz region. As a general rule, I am rarely impressed with any of its whites except semillon – although, in recent times, I've seen some good viogniers and even a promising albarino or two. I'm as likely to praise a Barossa chardonnay as I am to recommend anywhere in the region for a great coffee – other than Blond Coffee in Angaston. However, this chardonnay for Grant Burge's budget label came up looking good in a tasting for *Quaff* so I'm delighted to recommend it. The 2006 'Barossa Vines' Chardonnay is restrained, fine and surprisingly cool (rather than ripe) with good intensity, a pleasing savouriness and a crisp, dry, mouth-puckering finish. A modern style, great with food: say a spicy chicken salad or a Vietnamese chicken stir-fry.

2005 Haselgrove 'MVS' Chardonnay $15

This has abundant ripe tropical fruit flavours – typical of its warm McLaren Vale origins – along with some noticeable cedary oak. It has a good mouthfeel and is pleasant quaffing at a fair price.

2005 Jacob's Creek 'Reserve' Chardonnay $16.95

The attractive cedary oak dominates the aromas, but there's plenty of flavour, a core of ripe tropical fruit, creamy texture, some elegance and good length.

2006 Leasingham 'Circa 1893' Chardonnay $9

The Clare Valley makes Australia's best riesling, smart, often extraordinarily good shiraz, some flavourful cabernet and a handful of good semillons, grenaches and gewürztraminers. But it's not a region that does chardonnay particularly well. This budget-priced white from Leasingham is, however, a good, easy-drinking wine at a fair price. The 2006 'Circa 1893' Chardonnay has bright, ripe, sweet tropical fruit flavours, is clean and lively with refreshing, crisp acidity.

2006 Rosemount Estate 'Diamond Label' Chardonnay $15.95

There's little question that Rosemount has lost its way in the past few years. There have been some good wines under the label but compared to the excellent value-for-money wines that we've been used to, the winery's performance has been lacklustre. However, I'm pleased to say that I've been very impressed with the wine quality of the newly released Diamond Label wines, especially this Chardonnay and the 2005 Shiraz. Disappointingly, the price has crept a little over the $15 price point although I guess most will be able to buy this for less than $15 on special or by the case. The 2006 Diamond Label Chardonnay has impressive varietal character – persistent white peach and nectarine flavours, restrained oak, delightful viscosity and a clean, fresh finish. It's pleasingly bright and neatly balanced. A comeback worth watching.

 **GOOD**

2006 Card Collection Chardonnay $13.75

This is a Simon Gilbert label that is clean and fresh with concentrated melony flavours and a zesty finish.

2006 De Bortoli 'Deen Vat 7' Chardonnay $10.95

Here is a bold robust chardonnay from the Riverina that delivers heaps of oak and concentrated ripe peach flavour. Not for the faint-hearted.

2006 Four Sisters Chardonnay $14.30

The latest chardonnay of this successful label has attractive varietal character, is clean and fresh with good balance between its cool fruit and zippy acidity.

WHITE WINES UNDER $15

2006 Fox Creek 'Shadows Run' Chardonnay $12

The second label for the McLaren Vale's Fox Creek presents a supple, round, fine chardonnay with good varietal character, pleasant mouthfeel and ripe tropical notes.

2006 Little Rebel Chardonnay $17

Another second label – this time for the Yarra Valley's Punt Road that shown the region's deft touch with chardonnay: lively and fresh with intense white peach flavours and a good mouthfeel.

2006 Logan 'Apple Tree Flat' Chardonnay $10

I'm amazed at the ability of this family winery to produce such well-priced wines from Mudgee and Orange. This is uncomplicated, yet vibrant with intense, satisfying, fruit flavours.

2006 Long Flat 'Destinations' Chardonnay $14.95

From the team at Cheviot Bridge comes one of the best new labels around. This wine is sourced from the Yarra Valley and is fine with cool melony flavours, smooth almost creamy texture, and fresh, gentle acidity to finish.

2006 Preece 'White Label' Chardonnay $15.95

I'm not sure of the logic of Preece putting out two chardonnays – one at $14 and one at $16 – but I did like the more expensive wine, and not the other. Maybe there's my answer. This is thickly viscous, clean and lively with good weight, depth and refreshing stone-fruit flavours.

2006 Wolf Blass 'Red Label' Chardonnay $13.95

This is clean, fresh and well made with attractive fruity flavours.

CHARDONNAY

2006 X & Y Chardonnay $16.95

Here is another of the Evans & Tate chardonnays; this one is the responsibility of the X and Y generation winemakers – no Baby Boomer Chief Winemakers allowed here! The cedary oak is dominant but the clean, fresh fruity flavours are a match for it.

▶ PRETTY GOOD

2006 Back Vintage Chardonnay $11.95

Back Vintage has sourced a clean, fresh Hunter Valley chardonnay with good varietal character and some pleasant cedary oak. Mail order only.

2007 Gemtree 'Citrine' Chardonnay $14.95

Here is another McLaren Vale cheapie from one of the area's more impressive vineyards. This is well made with good ripe varietal character, a pleasant mouth-feel and clean fresh finish.

2006 Haselgrove 'Sovereign Series' Chardonnay $9.95

This is the cheaper of the two under-$15 labels of the McLaren Vale producer: soft, round and very easy to drink, good varietal character and a pleasant mouthfeel.

2006 McWilliam's 'Hanwood' Chardonnay $12

A gem from the Riverina that is one of the *Quaff* Reliables – it's been in every edition of this guide. That is consistency. In the tricky 2007 vintage, it's a decent, well-made chardonnay that feels good in the mouth, is clean, fresh, lively and easy to drink.

2006 Trentham Estate 'Murphy's Lore' Chardonnay $10

This is the budget-priced chardonnay from Trentham, more sherberty and sweeter than the other. Many will find it an attractive, easy-drinking chardonnay.

RIESLING

The popularity of riesling continues with, once again, a rise in the volume of the variety harvested in 2006. This is pushed by the strong demand for premium riesling which has resulted in an upward movement in the price of many of Australia's best quaffing rieslings. There's still heaps of great riesling available for less than $15 – in fact, the numbers received for the *Quaff* tastings are up by 25% this year.

We ask wineries to submit wines that are priced under $15 and that will be available from at least October to January. Those wineries that submit wines with a recommended retail price of more than $15 do so because they believe that the wine will be available in stores – at least on special – for below $15. Of the above-$15 wines I tasted I've only included the Tahbilk in this chapter; however, as with last year, there are ten value-for-money rieslings included in the chapter on Great-Value Wines over $15.

The reliables – consistent-quality wines, year in, year out

The rieslings from Peter Lehmann and Leasingham have appeared in seven out of the eight editions of *Quaff*. That's consistency!

Buying and Drinking Riesling – Some Tips

Drink young, fresh and vibrant ...

Most people enjoy rieslings when they are still in the first flush of youth (essentially within 18 months of harvest), when they are fragrant, fruity and lively with crisp dry acidity.

...or cellar for a few years

However, if you put riesling away in a cool dark place for a couple of years, it can develop some deliciously interesting bottle-age characters that are well worth exploring. Those with best cellaring potential include the 2007 Peter Lehmann Eden Valley or, from the Great-Value Wines over $15 chapter, the 2006 Frankland Estate 'Isolation Ridge' Riesling, the 2001 Heggies 'Reserve' Riesling, the 2006 Mountadam Riesling and the 2007 O'Leary Walker 'Polish Hill River' Riesling.

Rejoice in screwcap

The wholesale move away from cork – triggered in many ways by the united force of the Clare Valley's riesling producers who made a bold statement by rejecting cork en masse and moving to screwcap closures – has changed the face of the Australian wine industry. Cork taint, a dominant issue for wine writers and a major problem for the industry, has been dramatically reduced as the percentage of bottles sealed with cork decreases. As long as it's well cellared, riesling will age much better under screwcap.

Unfashionable value

As we say plenty of times in other parts of the book, if a wine is unfashionable expect it to be cheap. Although riesling is more fashionable than it was a few years ago, it is still unfashionable except with wine lovers. It represents amazing value – mainly thanks to the popularity of sauvignon blanc, sem sauv blanc blends and chardonnay.

WHITE WINES UNDER $15

▆▶ BLOODY GOOD

2007 Angove's 'Vineyard Select' Riesling $14.95

This is very good indeed. It's from a single vineyard in the Watervale area of Clare and has zesty lime aromas, is soft and intensely flavoured with pristine lime juice, lemon zest flavours before taut zingy acidity refreshes and cleanses the palate.

2007 Jim Barry Watervale Riesling $14.95

As happens each year, it's much easier to find good (even great) wines in the tastings of riesling. Wow, these were a joy with plenty of bargains to delight our palates. As expected the Clare and Eden valleys provided the stars with the Clare producer, Jim Barry, providing one of several 'Bloody Goods' from the tasting. The 2007 Jim Barry Watervale Riesling is a terrific regional wine: fresh, spotlessly clean with attractive fragrances, concentrated lemony, lime flavours before zesty acidity lifts and cleanses the palate.

2006 Leasingham 'Circa 1893' Riesling $10

I prefer this to its more expensive sibling, the 2006 Leasingham 'Magnus,' and believe it represents sensational value. It has wonderful talc aromas, is clean and remarkably fine for a wine at this price point, has pleasing limey, lemony flavours before a zippy, refreshing finish. I used the words 'poised' and 'focus' in my tasting notes which I would normally associate with more expensive whites. This is a quintessential quaffer – the kind of wine that *Quaff* is devoted to searching out and that my brother, Paul, would confidently serve with freshly caught whiting fillets and a squeeze of lime juice.

RIESLING

⭐ **2007 Peter Lehmann Eden Valley Riesling** $14.95
> THE 2008 OBERON KANT MEMORIAL AWARD FOR
> THE QUINTESSENTIAL QUAFFER,
> THE ULTIMATE AUSTRALIAN WINE UNDER $15 and
> THE QUAFF 2008 'Whooshable'
> WHITE WINE OF THE YEAR AWARD
>
> This is unbelievably good, with an ethereal floral bouquet and just a hint of talc, intense yet pure lemon, lime citrus flavours before a zesty, mouthwatering finish of significant length. There is finesse, elegance and more than a touch of class, too.

2007 Logan 'Weemala' Riesling $14.95
> This is sourced by the Logan family from a vineyard high (at 1000 metres) on the slopes of Mt Canobolas in the Orange region. The drought meant that yields in 2007 were absurdly low and so the wine has terrific concentration. There's some talc on the nose, juicy, intense, fresh lime juice flavours, impressive finesse, depth and length – and some pleasing softness to finish.

2006 Long Flat 'Destinations' Riesling $14.95
> This is an impressive Clare Valley riesling under the 'Destinations' badge of Cheviot Bridge's Long Flat label. It's intense, rich and concentrated with powerful lime zest acidity, and a touch of development showing. It's taut, mouth-puckering and zippy.

 **GOOD**

2006 Cookoothama Riesling $14.95
> Once again Nugan Estate's second label performs well, with a riesling that is sourced from its King Valley vineyard. It has gentle lemon zest, is fresh and lively with pleasing intensity of lemon citrus flavours and clean, zippy acidity.

WHITE WINES UNDER $15

2006 Peter Lehmann Barossa Riesling $12

This is a pleasant, easy-drinking riesling that is moderately concentrated with lemon citrus flavours and finishes with fresh, cleansing acidity.

2006 Peter Lehmann Eden Valley Riesling $14.95

Invariably one of Australia's best rieslings under $15 – and the 2006 doesn't disappoint. A whiff of talc on the nose, intense lemon citrus flavours and zesty acidity. Bright, clean and refreshing.

2005 Vintage Cellars Riesling $11.95

Excellent value from the guys at the supermarket chain: it's piercingly pure and fine with intense lemon, lime flavours and bright zippy acidity.

🍾 PRETTY GOOD

2007 Angove's 'Long Row' Riesling $9.95

A decent cheapie that is clean and fresh with distinct lemony flavours and a pleasing juiciness.

2006 Back Vintage Eden Valley Riesling $10.95

This well-made Eden Valley riesling doesn't have a great deal of concentration but has clean lemon citrus characters and fresh, gentle acidity.

2006 Bethany Riesling $14.95

There's gentle talc aromas and lively citrus flavours – a straightforward, undemanding quaffer.

2006 Leasingham 'Magnus' Riesling $13.95

This is a new range for the Clare Valley's Leasingham. I preferred its cheaper sibling, the 'Circa'. The 2006 'Magnus' is clean, fresh and well made, but lacks concentrated flavour and has noticeably high acidity.

2006 Tahbilk Riesling $16.45

This Nagambie Lakes riesling is lightly aromatic, fresh and clean with pleasant lemony flavours.

SAUVIGNON BLANC

Sauvignon is the trendy grape variety as Aussies continue their love affair and sales rise – especially in the cafes, bistros and brasseries. The Kiwis are doing amazing business over here, especially with their Marlborough sauvignons, which are well nigh impossible to beat at the price. Talk about fruit bombs! You should hear the Aussie wine marketers talk about Kiwis and their sauvignon blanc!

Australia's best sauvignon blancs tend to come from our cooler wine regions (where yields are lower and costs higher) and most of these are priced between $17 and $25. The best areas include the Adelaide Hills, Orange, Tasmania, the Alpine Valleys, the Grampians, Padthaway, (the south of) Margaret River and the Great Southern.

There are plenty of lacklustre or bland sauvignon blancs on the market at this price point. These tend to be clean and fresh yet lack clear varietal character or any concentration of flavour. Those rated 'Bloody Good' and 'Good' are light and bright with intense varietal flavours – even interest and excitement – and I'm delighted to be able to recommend them.

The reliables – consistent-quality wines, year in, year out

The Westend 'Richland' is one of the Reliables, having been reviewed in each edition of *Quaff*. It's a stunning performance as most of the other Riverina, or indeed warm-area, sauvignons lack intensity and concentration of flavour.

> ### Buying and Drinking Sauvignon Blanc – A Tip
>
> **Fresh and lively**
>
> The deadline for tastings has been kept as late as practical in the year to make it possible for wineries to present the current harvest's offerings. The pattern in *Quaff* has been for this chapter to be dominated by the most recent vintage. Last year, four out of the 14 recommended were not from the 2006 vintage and this year six out of 14 are not from 2007. For a 2006 sauvignon to have made this list, it would have to have retained its vibrance. As a general rule, however, this is a variety for drinking while it's fresh, young and lively.

 BLOODY GOOD

2006 Gnangara Sauvignon Blanc $10

This needed a bit of time and a good swirl to show its best, but is an excellent budget-priced sauvignon from the now defunct (but much lamented because the current wines are great!) Margaret River producer. Aromatic, intense tropical flavours, vibrant, creamy texture and zesty acidity.

2006 Long Flat 'Destinations' Sauvignon Blanc $14.95

This range first appeared under the Long Flat Wine Company label and has been rebadged. It offers regional varietals at surprisingly attractive prices. Of the current releases, I've been particularly impressed by the Barossa Shiraz and this Adelaide Hills Sauvignon. The latter is fragrant, showing intense and pure, cool green-skin fruit flavours with hints of gooseberries, finesse and elegance before some zesty racy acidity to finish.

2006 Printhie Sauvignon Blanc $15

I spent four days earlier in the year in Orange during their Food Week and enjoyed the hospitality, food and wines of this vibrant region. Printhie is owned by the Swift family and is based near Molong about half an hour's drive from Orange in the direction of Dubbo. More than any other winery from this cool-climate region (which means that it's expensive to produce grapes), Printhie focuses on budget-priced wines. I tasted through the line-up with winemaker Rob Black, and particularly liked this Sauvignon Blanc, the Pinot Gris and the Shiraz. The 2006 Printhie Sauvignon Blanc has restrained white stone-fruit characters, tropical notes, is plump on the mid-palate yet with tight structure, fresh zippy acidity and some passion-fruit lingering on a finish of moderate length. It is available in some retail outlets, mainly in New South Wales (check the website).

2007 Yalumba 'Y Series' Sauvignon Blanc $11.95

The Barossa-based Yalumba makes great value-for-money wines at many price points. At my first tasting of sauvignon blancs for *Quaff*, this was the pick of the bunch. Interestingly the Sauvignon Blanc from another of the Yalumba labels – Oxford Landing – was also a good performer. To be frank it requires skilful viticulture and clever winemaking to make decent sauvignon from warm areas. The 2007 Yalumba 'Y Series' Sauvignon Blanc is fresh, clean and vibrant, has cool tropical fruit flavours with some floral notes, and lively zippy acidity.

 **GOOD**

2007 Deakin Estate Sauvignon Blanc $10

This is the best I've seen from this Murray–Darling producer in some time. What a delicious, enticing wine is this: it's fresh, clean and vibrant with ripe tropical flavours and crisp, lively acidity and some passionfruit characters on its lingering finish.

2007 Oxford Landing Sauvignon Blanc $7.95

This is clean, fresh and lively with spicy, grapey flavours and hints of tropical fruits.

2006 Vintage Cellars Sauvignon Blanc $12.95

There's heaps of ripe tropical fruit here, juicy succulence and a lively tang, too.

2007 Westend 'Richland' Sauvignon Blanc $10.95

A drum roll for the Riverina's best and *Quaff*'s most consistent sauvignon blanc of all time. In 2007, it has that bright grassy, green bean character that heralds a crisp, clean, fruity wine.

SAUVIGNON BLANC

2006 X & Y Sauvignon Blanc $16

This is a Margaret River sauvignon (from the Evans & Tate young winemakers) with character that may well split opinion. It has intense green bean, green pea and fresh garden herb flavours, is cool, fresh and clean with intense, bracing acidity. Some will love the positive green characters while others may think they look under-ripe. The powerful acidity may also divide opinion.

▄▶ PRETTY GOOD

2007 Angove's 'Long Row' Sauvignon Blanc $9.95

I tasted this just after it had been bottled – and wines do take time to settle down. I particularly liked the palate and the mouthfeel so I'm confident that it will make a good quaffing wine.

2006 Commissioners Block Sauvignon Blanc $13.95

One of the labels for Roberts Estate; it has light, delicate floral aromas and some fresh, clean, tropical flavours.

2007 De Bortoli 'Deen Vat 2' Sauvignon Blanc $10.95

This is a decent quaffer that is fresh, clean and well made.

2007 Scarpantoni Sauvignon Blanc $18

This McLaren Vale sauvignon has some grassy characters and is straightforward and pleasant drinking.

2007 Zilzie 'Selection 23' Sauvignon Blanc $10

Again, I tasted this shortly after it had been bottled and so it wasn't looking at its best. I'm expecting some improvement by the time the book comes out. It's fresh and clean with some lingering tropical fruit flavours.

SEMILLON

This is a tiny section, mainly due to the decline in the number of semillons we are seeing for less than $15 a bottle. Australia is still producing heaps of semillon: it is second only to chardonnay in terms of volume of the variety produced (96 500 tonnes in 2006) and way ahead of riesling and sauvignon blanc. The success of semillon sauvignon blanc as a everyday drinking style means that that blend is much easier to market than varietal semillon.

As a varietal white, semillon is unique to Australia. The style of wine that it produces differs dramatically depending on the part of the country in which it is grown. In New South Wales' Hunter Valley it is a world-class wine that ages brilliantly. Lean, dry and often austere while young, it develops into a mellow, toasty, honeyed classic with time in the bottle. Interestingly, the Hunter vignerons are working hard at reinventing themselves and semillon and are looking to produce a more attractive, more marketable young wine than ever before. There's not much on the market under $15 but there are great examples here from Tulloch, McGuigan and Tyrrell's.

In South Australia's Barossa and Clare Valleys, semillon produces richer, fuller wines with more lemony flavours. In recent times, more wineries in these regions have been moving away from oaked semillons and making fresher, livelier, more drink-now styles. Western Australia's Margaret River and Great Southern produce a fresh, herbal, green pea, green bean style of semillon that has many admirers. The vast majority of these wines sell for more than $15 or are blended with sauvignon blanc to make a fresh, easy drink-now white blend, which is the only challenger to New Zealand sauvignon in cafes, brasseries and restaurants.

So, this may be a tiny section, but the wines reviewed are impressive.

The reliables – consistent-quality wines, year in, year out

The Hunter Valley's Tyrrell's and the Barossa's Peter Lehmann have been the leading producers of quaffing semillon and have been reviewed in seven of the eight editions of this annual guide. The McWilliam's favourite, Mount Pleasant 'Elizabeth', has crept up in price – at least in terms of its recommended retail price – so I've included it in the Great-Value Wines over $15 chapter. It is one of Australia's great wines, regardless of price.

Buying and Drinking Semillon – A Tip

Each way bets

One of the great things about semillon – especially from the Hunter Valley – is that it can be enjoyed while young for its fresh, lively, youthfulness or cellared for five to seven years and enjoyed for its mellow, toasty, honeyed flavours. Of the wines reviewed here, I think the Tyrrell's and the Peter Lehmann have the best ageing potential.

WHITE WINES UNDER $15

🍾 BLOODY GOOD

2007 McGuigan 'Bin 9000' Semillon $14.95

Here is an excellent example of the modern Hunter Valley style of semillon – and the proud winner of a gold medal at the 2007 Melbourne Wine Show. Not bad for a under-$15 white. It has lanolin and fresh hay aromas with some beguiling floral notes, is lively and fresh on the palate with intense lemon citrus flavours and zippy dry acidity.

2007 Tulloch Semillon $13

The Tulloch winery is performing brilliantly at present and is one of the places to visit when you're next in the Hunter Valley. This shows just what the region can do with fresh young, reasonably priced semillon. It has bright floral aromas, is vibrant, clean and juicy with fresh lanolin, straw and lemon citrus flavours before a lively fruity finish that lingers.

🍾 GOOD

2005 Peter Lehmann Semillon $14.95

Sales of the classic Peter Lehmann Semillon have been hit by the barrage of Kiwi sauvignons and so it's selling more slowly than usual – and they make substantial volumes of the wine. It retains its youthful zest and develops slowly so I've no hesitation in recommending it once again. Andrew Wigan and the team continue to show a deft touch with this consistently good, sometimes great, unoaked Barossa semillon. Not surprisingly they also picked up a trophy for their 2003 'Reserve' Semillon at the 2007 Melbourne Show. The 2005 Peter Lehmann Semillon is still looking fresh and bright with pristine, intense lemon citrus flavours, an attractive mouthfeel and zesty cleansing acidity.

2006 Torbreck 'Woodcutters' Semillon $18

Torbreck is one of the trendiest of the Barossa wineries and makes many sublime reds and this solitary dry white. While it is creeping up in price, it still represents great value: clean, fresh and dry with some lively lemon citrus flavours, an attractive mouthfeel, good weight and long, dry finish.

2006 Tyrrell's 'Old Winery' Semillon $12.95

The Melbourne Wine Show was a happy hunting ground for Tyrrell's, which won three gold medals for its 2007 semillons, including the expensive 'Vat 7', the cheap 2007 'Lost Block' and the next vintage of this delightful white. The 2006 has attractive dry, savoury characters with a great mouthfeel and zesty dry acidity to finish.

OTHER WHITE VARIETALS

The most popular varieties submitted for this section were verdelho, pinot grigio (and pinot gris), then viognier followed by chenin blanc. Pinot grigio is flavour of the month: it sells brilliantly in cafes, brasseries and restaurants and is being planted in substantially increased amounts. There was a 91% increase in its plantings (admittedly from a small base of 708 hectares) between 2005 and 2006. Interestingly, there are plenty of pinot grigios in the under-$15 price bracket, but fewer viogniers unless you pay more.

The reliables – consistent-quality wines, year in, year out

After eight editions of *Quaff*, only two wines have appeared in this chapter on each occasion: the Moondah Brook Verdelho and the Tahbilk Marsanne – consistently excellent value-for-money wines. The price of the Moondah Brook, along with pretty much everything in the Hardys portfolio, has gone up by a couple of dollars. I'm confident that it should be available on discount for less than $15 but will monitor the situation before next year's *Quaff*. So it may go the way of several of the Reliables that have crept out of our price bracket ... The Trentham Estate 'La Famiglia' Pinot Grigio is drawing attention to itself with its 'threepeat' or hat-trick of 'Bloody Goods'.

Buying and Drinking Other White Varietals – A Tip

Fresh is best

As usual, this chapter is dominated by whites from the most recent vintage. These tend to be unwooded and rely on freshness and vitality. Ripe, full-on flavours are very much part of the joy that the best of these wines can impart.

WHITE WINES UNDER $15

▶ BLOODY GOOD

2006 Angove's 'Nine Vines' Viognier $14

The Riverland's best producer has produced an excellent example of this variety. I've seen it on a number of occasions and liked very much each time. It has very attractive floral aromas, is lively, fresh and clean with delicate citrusy notes, good weight and viscosity before a crisp, dry finish.

2007 Capel Vale 'Debut' Chenin Blanc $14.95

There appears to be a significant lift in the Capel Vale wines this year, no doubt reflecting the influence of Larry Cherubino and some disciplined and skilful winemaking. I'm not a great fan of chenin blanc away from France's Loire Valley, but this is clean, fresh and floral, is soft, round and juicy, delicate yet intensely fruity and clearly focused.

2007 Logan 'Weemala' Pinot Gris $14.95

This is exceptional: and reflects the wine's sourcing from two vineyards – one at 650 metres and the other at 1000 metres – at Orange, so they are ultra-cool, and, because of the drought, from very low-yielding vines. There's a core of pristine flavour that threads through the wine – savoury with just a hint of pear skin and apple, wonderful thick viscosity and more power than you'd expect from an unwooded white. A wine of delicacy and finesse that finishes dry and long.

2007 Moondah Brook Verdelho $16.50

This has fragrant tropical fruit on the nose and this vibrant ripe flavour follows through on the palate. It is fresh, bright and intense with crisp, cleansing acidity on the finish. Straightforward and flavoursome.

OTHER WHITE VARIETALS

2007 Trentham Estate 'La Famiglia' Pinot Grigio $14.50

It's a hat-trick of BLOODY GOODs for the Murphy brothers, winemaker Anthony and viticulturist Pat, whose Trentham Estate is on a picturesque bend on the Murray just outside Mildura. There's a family resemblance to the previous year's Pinot Grigio in the 2007, which is delicate, fresh and clean, with subtle pear and apple flavours, some savouriness, good mouthfeel and a gentle easy-drinking finish.

2007 Tyrrell's 'Old Winery' Verdelho $12.95

I was in the Hunter Valley for the inaugural Hunter Valley Vignerons Legends Dinner. Half a dozen long-time servants of the region were inducted as Hunter Legends and Andrew Spinaze, Tyrrell's' long-serving winemaker (*Gourmet Traveller WINE*'s Winemaker of the Year in 2005) won this year's Hunter Valley Winemaker of the Year. Spinner is a great winemaker and a genius with Hunter semillon – and other white varieties. The 2007 vintage was tricky in most parts of the country: notable exceptions are the Hunter, the West and Tassie. This 'Old Winery' Verdelho is a pleasant Hunter Valley quaffer, attractively fruity, soft, round and generously flavoured with a touch of mid-palate fruit sweetness and lively acidity to finish.

2007 Westend 'Richland' Pinot Grigio $10.95

This is a terrific quaffer, but it's not what you expect of pinot grigio. In this case, I'm not sure it matters. The 2007 Richland Pinot Grigio has sweet tropical flavours, is aromatic, juicy and vibrant with clean ripe fruity flavours: easy to like.

WHITE WINES UNDER $15

 **GOOD**

2007 Angove's 'Long Row' Verdelho $9.95
This is an excellent example of a warm-climate verdelho: it's fruity, clean and fresh, with ripe sweet juicy fruit – very tropical.

2006 Peter Lehmann Chenin Blanc $12
As you'd expect from Andrew Wigan and the team at Peter Lehmann in the Barossa, this is clean and fresh with lively fruitiness and a pleasingly dry finish.

2006 McWilliam's 'Hanwood' Verdelho $12
This is soft, round, and very easy to drink, with good viscosity and some ripe apricotty flavours which linger.

2007 Tahbilk Marsanne $14.90
The omnipresent, ever-reliable Tahbilk Marsanne is sourced from a single vineyard that represents the world's largest planting of marsanne. It's refreshingly aromatic, zesty and vibrant with clean-cut fruity flavours that hint of cut grass and cool tropical characters before its zippy acidity presents a lively dry finish. One of the *Quaff* Reliables, present in every edition of the guide.

2007 Zilzie Pinot Grigio $14.95
There's the palest pink tinge to the wine, gentle savoury characters that are fresh and lively on the palate before a crisp, cleansing finish that lingers.

OTHER WHITE VARIETALS

🍾 PRETTY GOOD

2006 Commissioners Block Viognier $13.95

This is clean, fresh and well made, with gentle, delicate, savoury characters, pleasing viscosity and mouthfeel.

2006 T'Gallant 'Juliet' Pinot Grigio $13.95

From the Mornington Peninsula producer which turned Australians on to pinot grigio comes a budget-priced offering that is subtle, delicate and savoury, a very pleasant mouthfeel and crisp, lively acidity to finish.

2007 Yalumba 'Y Series' Pinot Grigio $11.95

This is more savoury than fruity, has a pleasing dry mouthfeel and gentle drying finish; serve it with a dish such as a Vietnamese chicken salad or stir fry and it comes into its own.

SEMILLON SAUVIGNON BLANC BLENDS

This is a relatively new style of wine that has made a huge impact on the Australian scene in the last decade or so. Its vibrance and drinkability has made it a huge favourite in cafes and brasseries across the country.

Margaret River winemakers claim that they invented this style, and I don't find it difficult to accept this. Semillon from that region has a grassy character that bears an amazing resemblance to sauvignon blanc, much more so than in other areas. Combining the two varieties seemed a natural thing to do as the weight, full body and complexity of semillon added a dimension to the vibrant juiciness of sauvignon blanc. The blend was a much more immediately satisfying drink than either of the two components. Because of its popularity and cost of production, most of the good examples of the blend from Margaret River have moved above $15 a bottle and their place has been taken by producers in the cooler areas of Western Australia – especially Pemberton and Frankland River – where the grapes are cheaper and, in many cases, zingier.

The important thing about this blend is having a fresh, zesty sauvignon blanc component. Many producers will get this by sourcing sauvignon blanc (or at least some of it) from a cool region. Those who rely on fruit from a warmer region will usually pick it early to retain the lively acidity that adds sparkle to the blend.

The popularity of the blend has led to imitators throughout Australia. Some are very smart wines. Others are very reasonably priced, as you'll see among those recommended in this chapter.

The reliables – consistent-quality wines, year in, year out

The Plantagenet 'Hazard Hill' Semillon Sauvignon Blanc has now appeared in seven of the last eight editions of *Quaff*, making it a reliable buy and consistent good value. The Houghton Semillon Sauvignon Blanc had been in six of the first seven editions but hadn't appeared from Houghton when the book went to print. That's a shame, as 2007 looks to be a brilliant year for these unwooded Houghton whites. Watch the *Quaff* website for further news.

Buying and Drinking Semillon Sauvignon Blanc Blends – A Tip

A quaffing good drink

I'm a great believer in drinking wines over a meal and there are plenty of light, uncomplicated dishes that are suited to accompanying semillon sauvignon blanc blends – summery salads, creamy pastas, Asian noodles and Chinese stir fries, especially with seafood or chicken. There will be times, however, when you may well want to relax with a refreshing glass of wine – on a quiet summer's afternoon or at a rowdy Friday night party – and this light, bright blend offers plenty of choice.

WHITE WINES UNDER $15

🍾 BLOODY GOOD

2007 De Bortoli 'Montage' Semillon Sauvignon Blanc $8.95

I felt quite buoyant after tasting the first batch of 28 sem sauv blancs for *Quaff*. The best shone. In spite of the trend towards higher prices, there will still be heaps of bargains at your favourite wine merchants into 2008. De Bortoli's cheapie 'Montage' has moved up a notch, adding consistency to outstanding performance and so underlining just why it was our 2007 Winery of the Year. This wine is a ripper: soft, round yet vibrant with intense ripe peach and melon flavours and a hint of spice and crisp, clean acidity on a finish which lingers. And the price! Need I say more.

2007 Ferngrove 'Symbols' Sauvignon Blanc Semillon $14.95

Frankland River may be a remote sub-region of the Great Southern but it has produced some extraordinary wines over the past few years. Kim Horton and his team have been leading the charge with brilliant, succulent reds and bright, vibrant whites. This blend often takes some time to show its best – but not in 2007. There are fragrant floral, sweet pea and lavender aromas, juicy refreshing cool tropical flavours and bracing, crisp natural acidity.

2007 Firestick Semillon Sauvignon Blanc $14.95

This is the best wine I've seen from the second label of the Hunter Valley's Poole's Rock. It is clean, fresh and lively with floral aromas, gentle, ripe, tropical fruit and some juiciness before a vibrant zesty finish featuring gentle green pea characters.

2007 Four Sisters Sauvignon Blanc Semillon $14.30

A delicious white blend from this popular label that was originally linked to Mt Langi Ghiran. This is soft and round with ripe sweet, peach and juicy tropical flavours and fresh, zippy acidity which cleanses the palate.

SEMILLON SAUVIGNON BLANC BLENDS

2006 Growers 'Peppermint Grove' Sauvignon Blanc Semillon $14.95

Made at Bruce Duke's Naturaliste Vintners in Margaret River, this is an exceptional and well-priced example of the style: fragrant, fresh and pristine with ripe, intense tropical flavours and gentle, zesty acidity.

2007 Hanging Rock 'Rock' Semillon Sauvignon Blanc $14

The extensive Hanging Rock range of John and Ann Ellis offers many sublime wines including my favourite, the vibrant Hanging Rock 'Jim Jim' Sauvignon Blanc. This 2007 Sem Sauv Blanc is the best of Hanging Rock's budget-priced 'Rock' label – fresh, clean and lively, succulent and juicy with cool intense tropical fruit flavours and bright, refreshing acidity. It's a satisfying cool-climate drink-me-now white at a fair price.

2006 Tatachilla 'Growers' Semillon Sauvignon Blanc $12.95

Fanchon Ferrandi continues to do excellent work at this popular McLaren Vale winery. As you'd expect from a winery that sources most of its fruit from this warm region, I've preferred the budget-priced reds – under the 'Keystone' and 'Partners' labels – to the whites. This is the best 'Growers' white blend I've seen from Tatachilla: it has more depth and varietal character than the previous five vintages of the wine. The 2006 Growers is clean, fresh and delightfully tropical; tight, lean and lively, finishing with crisp racy acidity.

2007 Willow Bridge Sauvignon Blanc Semillon $15.50

David Crawford is making some exceptional whites from the Ferguson Valley's largest producer. This has delightful sweet pea florals, ripe tropical flavours that are clean, vibrant and refreshing in the mouth before a long, cool finish with green pea flavours that linger.

2007 Woodstock Semillon Sauvignon Blanc $14.95

Don't ask me how Scott Collett, Ben Glaetzer and the team at this revitalised McLaren Vale winery made a white wine this good. The region does brilliant reds (especially shiraz) but I usually find it too warm for whites. This is refreshingly fragrant, shows bright ripe passionfruit and tropical fruit flavours and wonderful vibrance before a finish which features crisp, cleansing acidity. Great price, too.

 GOOD

2006 Anvers Semillon Sauvignon Blanc $16

The McLaren Vale-based producer, Anvers, has sourced grapes for this fresh fruity white blend from the Adelaide Hills, so guaranteeing greater intensity of more vibrant, cool fruit. There are white peach and passionfruit flavours and lively, zesty acidity, too.

2007 Catching Thieves Semillon Sauvignon Blanc $15.95

McWilliam's has been involved in Margaret River for some time but the Catching Thieves label is a sign of a more intense, long-term commitment to the region. The freshness and vibrance of the Margaret River fruit is evident here, as is the liveliness of the mouthfeel and the clean, crisp finish.

2007 O'Leary Walker 'Blue Cutting Road' Sauvignon Blanc Semillon $14.95

Here is a new label for the Clare Valley-based team of David O'Leary and Nick Walker that succeeds, at least, with this wine. The nose is more gewürztraminer, with perfumed spice, rose petal and florals, yet the flavours and mouthfeel are very much sauv blanc sem. There's a liveliness on the mid-palate, ripe tropical flavours and a cleansing, refreshing finish.

SEMILLON SAUVIGNON BLANC BLENDS

2006 Plantagenet 'Hazard Hill' Semillon Sauvignon Blanc $12

As you'll see from the introduction to this section, the Hazard Hill is one of the most consistent quaffers on the market. In the fairly difficult 2006 vintage, it still did well thanks to its freshness, clean, lively tropical flavours, easy drinkability and crisp zesty acidity.

2007 Skuttlebutt Sauvignon Blanc Semillon $16

Janice McDonald and the team at Margaret River's Stella Bella must be delighted with the quality of the last two vintages of this cheapie. In 2007, it's vibrant, pristine and wildly refreshing, packed with ripe passionfruit, guava and nectarine flavours and finishes long and satisfying.

2007 Watershed 'Shades' Sauvignon Blanc Semillon $15.95

This large, investor-driven vineyard and winery is situated to the south of Margaret River and so you can expect refreshing cool whites such as this sauv blanc sem blend. It's an easy-drinking style with ripe sweet fruit flavours and lingering passionfruit to finish.

PRETTY GOOD

2006 Alkoomi Semillon Sauvignon Blanc $15.80

Frankland River's longest serving producer has made a clean fresh white blend that has lively lemon citrus and grapefruit flavours.

2006 Barking Owl Semillon Sauvignon Blanc $16.50

This is the second label of Perth Hills producer Millbrook. The wine is clean and well made with some decent fruity flavours.

2007 Capel Vale 'Debut' Sauvignon Blanc Semillon $14.95

A lively, clean white blend that shows pleasing varietal character.

WHITE WINES UNDER $15

2007 De Bortoli 'Windy Peak' Sauvignon Blanc Semillon $14.95
> Attractive aromas and ripe, sweet tropical fruit flavours that linger.

2007 Haselgrove 'Sovereign Series' Semillon Sauvignon Blanc $9.95
> A McLaren Vale white blend that drinks easily and is clean, fresh and cheap.

2006 Leaping Lizard Semillon Sauvignon Blanc $15
> The Ferngrove second label sometimes gives its sibling a hiding. While that's not the case, this year, the Leaping Lizard has intense tropical flavours and an appealing mouthfeel.

2006 Logan 'Apple Tree Flat' Semillon Sauvignon Blanc $10
> Clean, fresh and splashy (OK, even I am not sure what that means), just a bit dilute. Still pleasant drinking at a good price.

2007 McWilliam's 'Inheritance' Semillon Sauvignon Blanc $7
> A pleasant inoffensive Riverina white blend for those occasions when you don't want to think or pay too much.

2006 Poet's Corner Semillon Sauvignon Blanc $9.95
> Still fresh and lively with uncomplicated cool tropical flavours and crisp, dry acidity.

2007 Trentham Estate 'Two Thirds' Semillon Sauvignon Blanc $12.50
> I've loved this low-alcohol white blend for the past two years. While I like its easy drinkability and bold acidity, this doesn't have the depth of flavour of the previous vintages.

SEMILLON SAUVIGNON BLANC BLENDS

2007 Tulloch Semillon Sauvignon Blanc $13

> This Hunter Valley white has easy drinkability, a good mouthfeel and a decent aftertaste.

2007 Tyrrell's 'Old Winery' Semillon Sauvignon Blanc $12.95

> Another top Hunter producer with a pleasant, well-made wine from a very good vintage.

2007 Vino Gusto Semillon Sauvignon Blanc $5.95

> While this doesn't have a great deal of character it's surprisingly pure, feels great in the mouth, and is unlikely to break the bank.

OTHER WHITE BLENDS

I said it last year and I'm saying it again. I found the tasting for this section pretty hard work. The fact of the matter is that because of the price point that is being targeted, these are bin-end wines. So everything goes into the blend – and I get to taste the most amazing combinations imaginable. The bonus is that, although the tasting (overall) was disappointing, the top wines were once again terrific.

Especially in this section, blind tastings are a significant part of *Quaff*. As I don't know what the blends are until after I have finished making notes on the wines and rating them, I can't be put off by my expectations of what a seemingly bizarre combination of grapes might produce. Surprise packets to impress include the 2007 Primo Estate 'La Biondina' Colombard Sauvignon Blanc, 2006 De Bortoli 'Sero' Chardonnay Pinot Grigio and the 2006 Sandalford 'Element' Chenin Blanc Verdelho Semillon.

Thank goodness Australian appellation laws allow for blending literally any grape from anywhere with any other grape from anywhere else. What is pleasing, too, is that these blends still express a good sense of where they're from – whether it be the grassy, fresh, perfumed quality of the Western Australian blends or the ripe, rich flavours of the warmer-climate South Australian wines.

It's time to announce the demise of the Semillon Chardonnay section. With the popularity of Semillon Sauvignon Blanc blends, winemakers are not prepared to sacrifice semillon for the fairly unfashionable Sem Chardonnays and so this category has all but disappeared from retailers' shelves. We had only six wines entered this year; the Peter Lehmann Semillon Chardonnay was rated Good, and four others Pretty Good. So these are included in this section.

The reliables – consistent-quality wines, year in, year out

Only two wines in this chapter have appeared in all eight editions of *Quaff* – the Primo Estate 'La Biondina' Colombard Sauvignon Blanc and the Rosemount Estate 'Diamond Cellars' Semillon Chardonnay. 'La Biondina' has moved to this section from Other White Varietals – where it shone as a straight colombard. In 2004 and 2005 it was labelled a blend of colombard, sauvignon blanc and riesling and now it's colombard sauvignon blanc. The Rosemount Estate white has appeared in the Semillon Chardonnay section until this year.

Buying and Drinking Other White Blends – Some Tips

Fresh is best

There is no question that the fresher these blends are the better they are. All these wines are either from 2005 or 2006. They need to be drunk up before they are two years old, when their fruit flavours are at their liveliest and brightest. In fact, they are generally at their best before they have had their first birthday.

Summertime blues

The best of these blends make great uncomplicated summertime drinking and are being sourced from many parts of Australia rather than, as previously, along the banks of the mighty River Murray. This variety in the places from which they are sourced means that you have greater choice in the styles you drink than before. If you want a dry white blend, it's available.

BLOODY GOOD

2006 De Bortoli 'Sero' Chardonnay Pinot Grigio $13.95

De Bortoli continues its winning ways with excellent wines coming from their winery in the Riverina at Griffith and from the Yarra Valley property at Dixon's Creek. The 'Sero' wines are sourced from the King Valley and made in the Yarra by Steve Webber and his brilliant team of young winemakers. I tasted this with a range of wines which are labelled Other White Blends (that is, not semillon sauvignon blanc) in *Quaff*. Steve Webber and his team are more interested in building texture than varietal flavour and that seems to me admirably suited to crafting an interesting wine from a blend of varieties like chardonnay and pinot grigio. Don't expect obvious varietal fruit flavours. This is a wine that has weight, power, impressive depth and viscosity with a delightful mouthfeel and a wonderfully dry finish. An excellent food white: say with Vietnamese or Thai chicken stir fries or even grilled fish and chips.

2007 Houghton White Classic $10.50

It's the 70th consecutive vintage of the Houghton White Burgundy (given the pathetic name of White Classic by the marketers when Australia had to stop using protected European names); it's still a huge seller and consistently a great quaffing white. The 2007 vintage was brilliant in the Swan, from which more than 80% of the blend comes, so this will be an outstanding example of the style. It's a blend of chenin blanc (50%) with chardonnay, verdelho, muscadelle and a touch of semillon. The 2007 Houghton White Classic is lively, intense, pristine, fruity, has a great mouthfeel and a zesty clean finish.

OTHER WHITE BLENDS

2007 Parri Viognier Chardonnay $18

Parri is newish winery from the Fleurieu Peninsula that produces some interesting wines like this delightfully fragrant, clean, fresh and floral white blend. It is soft and round, has a pleasing mouthfeel and ripe, sweet fruit flavours that linger. Delicious.

2007 Primo Estate 'La Biondina' Colombard Sauvignon Blanc $14.95

Joe Grilli and the Primo Estate team are now based in McLaren Vale although he still sources plenty of the colombard from his previous home on the Adelaide Plains. I love the way this shines every year in the tastings for *Quaff*, standing out like the proverbial beacon. This year, I love its ripe sweet tropical fruit and passionfruit flavours, vibrance, succulent and crisp, refreshing, zesty acidity.

2007 Sandalford 'Element' Classic White $12.95

This blend continues the outstanding quality reached by Sandalford and winemaker, Paul Boulden, with this wine from the previous vintage. And so it should, as 2007 was a fantastic year in Western Australia. It's again a blend of chenin blanc, verdelho, semillon and some bin ends that works extraordinarily well: delightfully aromatic with fresh garden herb flavours, mid-palate juiciness, and some sweet pea florals lingering on the finish.

 **GOOD**

2007 Gemtree 'Tadpole' Chardonnay Viognier $14.95

Here is a McLaren Vale blend that works well. It's intense, packed with flavours, thick, dry and textural, finishing long and satisfying.

WHITE WINES UNDER $15

2006 Peter Lehmann Semillon Chardonnay $12

> The ever-reliable Peter Lehmann team has produced a vibrant, bright white blend that is fruity and succulent yet quite chewy, finishing with a satisfying dryness.

🍾 PRETTY GOOD

2007 Angove's 'Butterfly Ridge' Colombard Chardonnay $6.95

> A fresh, bright and lively unwooded style from the Riverland: some grassy characters and appealing mouthfeel.

2006 Brown Brothers 'Everton' Chardonnay Sauvignon Blanc Pinot Gris $13.50

> Here is a gentle, delicate white blend that is fresh and well-made with pleasant fruity flavours.

2007 Coriole Chenin Blanc $13.95

> Not many whites work well in the warmth of McLaren Vale. Coriole, however, have a long-established reputation for chenin blanc. In 2007, it is fresh, clean and fruit with ripe, sweet tropical fruit and lively zippy acidity.

2006 De Bortoli 'Sacred Hill' Semillon Chardonnay $6.50

> This is a cheapie with grassy, straw characters and a pleasant dry finish.

2006 De Bortoli 'Sacred Hill' Traminer Riesling $6.50

> Dramatic spicy, rose petal nose typical of gewürztraminer, more viscous and smoothly textured than you'd expect. Finish fresh, crisp and dryish.

2006 De Bortoli 'Sacred Hill' Unwooded Colombard Chardonnay $6.50

> Uncomplicated yet lively and fresh with good viscosity and vibrance and a clean, refreshing finish.

OTHER WHITE BLENDS

2007 Jane Brook 'Plain Jane' Chardonnay Chenin Blanc $13.50
Sourced from the Swan Valley, this has attractive floral aromas and pleasant fruity flavours.

2006 Penfolds 'Rawsons Retreat' Semillon Chardonnay $10.95
A soft, round, easy-drinking style.

2006 Queen Adelaide Semillon Chardonnay $7.95
There are some gentle, almost honeyed characters on the nose yet the wine is savoury rather than fruity, with good weight and a pleasing dry finish.

2006 Rosemount Estate 'Diamond Cellars' Semillon Chardonnay $11.95
This has savoury rather than fruity flavours and is clean, fresh, even vibrant, with an appealing dry finish that lingers.

2006 Sticks Chardonnay Viognier $13.95
An unwooded Yarra Valley blend that has refreshing zesty cool flavours and lively acidity.

Blushing beauties
Pink wines under $15

PINK WINES UNDER $15

The rosé revolution continues and, if anything, has gathered more force in the past 12 months. It has swept rosé to a prominence only dreamt of by a few visionaries until recently. Interestingly, the trend is international, with the significant British wine market taking to the pink drop with the same zeal as wine lovers in Australia.

Below $15, the majority of rosés have some residual sugar. This style is enormously popular. The challenge for me is to differentiate between those rosés that have a small amount of residual sugar to flesh them out, smoothen the palate, and to make them easier to drink, and those which have residual sugar to make them sweet. The latter often fail by being too sweet and cloying. If you prefer your rosés dry, as I do, you'll still find some to please you in this chapter.

Like so many of the wines that are produced to be drunk early, screwcaps are becoming increasingly prevalent. I applaud the continued use of screwcaps with almost all rosés (all but two received for this chapter). This means that vibrant youthful freshness will be part of your experience of drinking rosé.

> **THE QUAFF 2008 'Run for the Roses'**
> **PINK WINE OF THE YEAR AWARD**
> On the shortlist for this award are:
> 2007 Angove's 'Nine Vines' Grenache Shiraz Rosé
> 2007 De Bortoli 'Sero' Cabernet Rosato
> 2007 Innocent Bystander Moscato
> 2006 Jacob's Creek 'Three Vines' Shiraz Grenache Sangiovese
>
> Angove's has worked hard on rosé in the vineyard and the winery; it has decided that Riverland shiraz and grenache picked early are ideal for rosé and the judges at last year's National Show agreed. Angove's has continued the good work in 2007. I also love the style of the De Bortoli and the company's consistency with this style. I know that the Innocent Bystander Moscato isn't in this chapter but it is pink, Australia's best example of the style and quite delicious. The Jacob's Creek 'Three Vines' is a surprise packet, an excellent example of the style, and the kind of rosé that Australians will love. It's the *Quaff 2008* Pink Wine of the Year.

The reliables – consistent-quality wines, year in, year out

Australia's pink wines have not proved to be all that consistent over the years. A couple of the more consistent wines have crept out of our price bracket – including the Geoff Merrill Grenache Rosé (though his Mount Hurtle is a bargain at $8) and the Wandin Valley 'Pavilion'. They still represent good value.

Just to prove the point about consistency, the most consistent rosé of the past three years, the Scarpantoni 'Ceres' Rosé, didn't come up brilliantly in our tasting this year. The Angove's 'Nine Vines' Grenache Shiraz Rosé (trophy winner at the 2006 National Wine Show in Canberra) and the De Bortoli 'Sero' Cabernet Rosato have been the most consistent performers in this price range in the past couple of years.

Buying and Drinking Pink Wines – Some Tips

Fresh is best

I'm a great believer that rosés are best drunk young. A healthy majority (10 out of 15) of the recommended rosés in this year's *Quaff* are from the current vintage, which means that they will be wonderfully fresh.

Now that the revolution is here

While more rosés are more widely available in Australia than ever before, this is not time for complacency. Support those winemakers who have been overwhelmed by the tide of public opinion and given us what we wanted. More choice: more rosés. Continue supporting the rosé push!

PINK WINES UNDER $15 99

▶ BLOODY GOOD

2007 Angove's 'Nine Vines' Grenache Shiraz Rosé $14.95

Last year this developed a more savoury character with about six months' bottle age, so I wonder if that will happen again. At present, it has more fruitiness than I remember the 2006 having: strawberry, red cherry and raspberry flavours. It is soft, round and very easy to drink (thanks to the low 12.5° alcohol) is ripe, plump and juicy with gentle dry acidity to cleanse the palate.

2007 De Bortoli 'Sero' Cabernet Rosato $14.95

The cabernet is sourced from De Bortoli's King Valley vineyard and the wine is made in a very modern style. In 2007, it's restrained, fine, lean and tight with a savoury edge and a silky smooth dry finish. Delicious.

★ **2006 Jacob's Creek 'Three Vines' Shiraz Grenache Sangiovese** $14.95

THE QUAFF 2008 'Run for the Roses'
PINK WINE OF THE YEAR AWARD

Here is a new quaffing label from the Pernod Ricard team, badged like almost everything else as Jacob's Creek, and offering a terrific rosé. The blend is clever, combining the Barossa's two great strengths – shiraz and grenache – with the Tuscan cultivar sangiovese, which should add some savoury notes to the wine. This has restrained aromatics, is soft and round with vibrant strawberry and redcurrant flavours and a crisp, clean, fresh finish and delicious aftertaste.

2007 Moondah Brook Rosé $12.50

This is made from cabernet sauvignon, has a rose petal fragrance, ripe strawberry flavours, is very soft on the mid-palate and has a crisp, clean finish with a touch of sweetness.

PINK WINES UNDER $15

2006 Sirromet '820 Above' Rosé $14.95

Queensland's largest producer with an excellent cellar door and superb restaurant at Mt Cotton, 45 minutes' drive from Brisbane, has the '820 Above' range of wines from the Granite Belt to emphasise its altitude. Given its latitude, it's that height above sea level that enables the region to produce some smart wines. This is a serious rosé that is soft, round and easy to drink yet shows restraint, a lean, tight structure, savouriness and a balanced, bone-dry finish.

2006 Yalumba 'Y Series' Sangiovese Rosé $11.95

The pursuit of excellence is alive and well at Yalumba. Here's another gem from the budget-priced 'Y Series': clean, fresh and restrained with tangy redcurrant and red cherry flavours and balanced zippy acidity on a dry, savoury finish.

 **GOOD**

2006 Mount Hurtle Grenache Rosé $8

An uber-budget-priced rosé from the Geoff Merrill team in the McLaren Vale. It has restrained savoury characters, is smooth and viscous before a pleasantly dry finish. Suited to lightly spiced Thai stir-fries of fish or chicken.

2007 Sandalford 'Protege' Rosé $18.95

Look to get this very pleasant Western Australian rosé on special. It's sweet and round in the mouth with strawberry and red cherry flavours, some weight on the mid-palate and balanced by gentle acidity.

2007 Willow Bridge Rosé $15.50

Willow Bridge is situated in the stunningly picturesque Ferguson Valley (in the Geographe region) with fabulous hillside views over the hinterland towards the coastal town of Bunbury. The 2007 has light crimson-pink colour, sweet musk stick, even lipstick, and strawberry flavours. That sweetness is quite restrained and its fresh, cleansing acidity leaves a dry aftertaste.

▶ PRETTY GOOD

2007 McPherson Cabernet Rosé $10.95

This is a soft, round and easy-drinking style that is sweet without being overwhelmingly so. There's strawberry and raspberry fruit pastille with a hint of musk stick.

2007 Scarpantoni 'Ceres' Rosé $14

This is made from gamay from the McLaren Vale and is often Australia's best-value rosé. The growing conditions for the 2007 vintage were extremely difficult and this has probably contributed to Scarpantoni producing a decent rather than terrific 'Ceres'. These guys won the Jimmy Watson Trophy for their 2006 Scarpantoni 'Brothers Block' Cabernet Sauvignon ($25–$30) so we don't need to feel too sorry for them. I find the 2007 'Ceres' soft, round, sweet and fruity – a bit too sweet for me. It's pleasant drinking but without its usual depth.

Sweet Nicoli $11.95

I'm in at least two minds about this sweetie from All Saints at Rutherglen. It has confectionery and pink musk stick aromas, powerful lolly-like flavours and a pleasant sweet finish. Part of me thinks it might be sweet but not too sweet and part of me thinks it is way too sweet. If you like pretty sweet, give it a try.

2007 Trentham Estate 'La Famiglia' Sangiovese Rosé $14.50

This is pleasantly uncomplicated and sweet yet with a savoury edge on the finish thanks to the sangiovese grape.

2007 Wirra Wirra 'Mrs Wigley' Rosé $16.50

I can't imagine that winemaker Sam Connew's chocolate labrador, Mercy Brown, would have been all that impressed that she has made a rosé named after a cat, even if it's the (former) winery cat, Mrs Wigley. Still, that's life. This is soft, round and very easy drinking, silky smooth and sweet. It is in balance, gentle and pleasing on the palate – just a bit too sweet for me but bound to be very popular. Now if it were named after a dog, that might be different.

2007 Woodstock Rosé $14.95

This is a blend that is predominantly grenache and predominantly from the McLaren Vale. It is consistently in the sweeter spectrum. For me, this is a bit more commercial than last year's – with raspberry and boiled lolly flavours and more sweetness. However, if you like sweetness …

Barbecue wines

Red wines under $15

RED WINES UNDER $15

THE QUAFF 2008 'Fillet Steak and Chips'
RED WINE OF THE YEAR AWARD

On the shortlist for this award are:
2005 Capel Vale 'Debut' Merlot
2006 De Bortoli 'Windy Peak' Pinot Noir
2005 Ferngrove 'Symbols' Cabernet Merlot
2006 Red Knot Shiraz
2006 Schild Estate Grenache Mataro Shiraz
2006 Yalumba 'Y Series' Shiraz Viognier

The Schild Estate Grenache Mataro Shiraz and the Red Knot Shiraz are gorgeous examples of quaffing reds, seductively textured, slurpable and begging to be drunk young. The Ferngrove 'Symbols' Cabernet Merlot is more of an each-way bet – drinkable now but with cellaring potential, and more than a touch of elegance and power. The Capel Vale 'Debut' Merlot and the De Bortoli 'Windy Peak' Pinot add a touch of restraint and complexity to the picture and help transform the category of quaffing wines. Both are bewilderingly good examples of brilliant winemaking taming notoriously tricky varieties and both are worthy of a place at the finest dinner party. Match these six wines against similarly priced wines from any wine-producing country in the world and you'd see just how great is the potential of the Australian wine industry.

Choosing between the Capel Vale, the De Bortoli and the Yalumba 'Y Series' Shiraz Viognier is no easy task. The previous vintage of the Yalumba was the *Quaff* Wine of the Year in 2007, so you could say that it's had its turn. The 2006 Yalumba Shiraz Viognier, however, is a simply splendid red that is the essence of quaffability. It's my *Quaff 2008* Red Wine of the Year.

THE QUAFF 2008 'Sausages and Chips'
BEST RED WINE UNDER $10 AWARD

On the shortlist for this award are:
2006 Angove's 'Long Row' Cabernet Sauvignon
2005 Angove's 'Stonegate' Petit Verdot
2004 Leasingham 'Circa 1893' Shiraz Cabernet
2005 Wolf Blass 'Eaglehawk' Cabernet Sauvignon

I've raved about the 'Stonegate' Petit Verdot on several occasions during the year but the guys from Angove's tell me that petit verdot just doesn't sell and they suspect that they won't be making the wine again. I can't believe this, as it's bold, full of flavour and quaffable. The Leasingham 'Circa 1893' Shiraz Cabernet is a terrific Clare quaffer from a new cheaper range from Hardys. The 'Eaglehawk' is Wolf Blass at its most slurpable, a very good flavour-packed red that begs to be drunk young.

I've gone for the 2006 Angove's 'Long Row' Cabernet Sauvignon as Best Red Wine under $10 because of its beguiling flavours (amazing in a wine at this price point), its superb texture and impeccable balance.

CABERNET SAUVIGNON

There appears to have been some improvements in the quality and approachability of cabernets at this price point over the past few years. I used to find that cabernet's high levels of tannin (the drying grippiness you feel on the sides of your tongue and gums) made the wines sturdy, even confronting – especially when compared to more supple, fleshy, and less firmly tannic varieties such as shiraz and grenache. There appears more approachability and an easing off in the use of oak which makes the wines easier to love – or at least cuddle.

Cabernet sauvignon has declined in popularity in the last few years and is certainly a much harder sell now than it used to be. The reality is that it is one of the classic wines of the world, does particularly well in many parts of Australia, and makes many brilliant wines – at all price points. That's why the best wines in the chapter are well worth considering. I've talked to plenty of producers in the past year who've admitted that they've dropped the price of their cabernet in order to get consumers interested in it. It's a well-worn Quaff notion that if something is unfashionable, it is likely to represent much better value than something that is trendy.

The reliable – consistent-quality wines, year in, year out

Still the nation's most consistent cabernet sauvignon at this price point is the popular Lindemans 'Bin 45', which has appeared in seven out of eight editions of *Quaff* and remains good value.

Buying and Drinking Cabernet Sauvignon – Some Tips

Short-term cellaring

Most cabernets made at this price point are designed to be approachable so that they can be consumed young. As a general rule, if they are priced below $10 they won't drink any better than they will when you buy them. They should be drunk within six months or so – although they may last perfectly well for longer. If they are priced above $10, they may well benefit from short-term cellaring (six months to a year or two) as they are likely to mellow a bit and become an even better drink. If you are going to cellar some wine, store it in the coolest, darkest room you can find – ideally one without much temperature variation. You'll find that the better the storage conditions, the longer you can keep the wine.

Cabernet sauvignon and food

I generally drink wine with food. If I were to be drinking a red wine at a party or in some situation without food, I would avoid cabernet sauvignon. I'd be looking for something much gentler. With food, however, it's a different matter. Cabernet can be transformed by food. It appears much softer, more supple, even more mellow – those tannins appear to be gulped up by the wine. Best matches include full-flavoured meat dishes – steak, roast lamb, venison or kangaroo fillets, especially served with robust sauces – and hard cheeses such as parmesan or cheddar. Appropriate matches can include casseroles such as lamb shanks, osso buco or coq au vin – especially if you can slip a bit of the wine into the dish.

RED WINES UNDER $15

🍾 BLOODY GOOD

⭐ 2006 Angove's 'Long Row' Cabernet Sauvignon $9.95
THE QUAFF 2008 'Sausages and Chips'
BEST RED WINE UNDER $10 AWARD

The Riverland's big improver has made a classically unpretentious quaffer that drinks beautifully – very soft and fruity with redcurrant and blackcurrant flavours, succulent and silky smooth texture, neat balance and supple gentle finish. Quaff on!

2006 Deakin Estate Cabernet Sauvignon $10

If Angove's is turning my head with the quality of its Riverland wines, Deakin Estate is doing the same in the Murray–Darling, where they are perched at Red Cliffs near Mildura. (Actually Red Cliffs seems pretty flat to me, I'd better do a more comprehensive tour of the landscape next time I'm in the region.) This is clean, fresh and well made, has deep, ripe redcurrant, dark plum and cassis flavours, is fleshy, generous and so approachable – just how we like our cabernets at this price.

2004 Koonara 'Angel's Peak' Cabernet Sauvignon $14.95

The Reschkes have lived and farmed in Coonawarra for more than 100 years, having arrived in 1906. Trevor and Vivian Reschke have two sons, Burke who produces wines under the Reschke label, and Dru who is responsible for Koonara. Winemaker for Koonara is long-term Coonawarra resident Peter Douglas who made a name for himself at Wynns. Angel's Peak is the budget label of Koonara and offers Coonawarra cabernet and shiraz at modest prices. The 2004 vintage is proving exceptional in the region so you'd expect some value from even the cheaper reds. There's some vanilla bean and cedary oak notes in the 2004 'Angel's Share' Cabernet, dense, deep, ripe blackcurrant and dark plum flavours, tight structure and quite firm, though not aggressive tannins. It will improve over the short term but will be greatly enhanced by food – perhaps a hearty, slow-cooked beef stew.

2005 Preece Cabernet Sauvignon $14.95

Instead of having the public regard Preece as a second label for Mitchelton, Lion Nathan has moved to establish it as a stand-alone entity. So this is the last vintage to bear the Mitchelton name. I preferred it to the 2006 for its smoothness and approachability. It features ripe redcurrant, dark plum and blackcurrant flavours, velvety texture and moderate, balanced tannins. Worth searching for.

2005 Rex Watson Cabernet Sauvignon $14.95

Here's a quality newcomer. The Watson Wine Group has very quickly become a major player in Coonawarra – it describes the company as the largest independent grape grower in the region with a potential production of 400 000 cases. They now have more than 400 hectares in three vineyards close to the Coonawarra township. The budget-priced Rex Watson range is the first releases. The 2005 Rex Watson Shiraz won Blue Gold at the Sydney International Top 100, although my preference is for this Cabernet. It's made by Roger Harbord, who was Chief Winemaker at Normans and now has his own brand. The 2005 Rex Watson Cabernet is soft, round and very approachable; has bright, persistent, redcurrant and red cherry flavours, smooth attractive texture and ripe, balanced tannins.

2005 Wolf Blass 'Eaglehawk' Cabernet Sauvignon $10

From looking at the 'Bloody Goods' in this section you can get an idea of the style of cabernets that I believe look (that is, taste) best at this price point. And the Eaglehawk exemplifies the style: it's juicy, almost syrupy, has rich dark berry flavour with good concentration and a soft, gentle finish. Most importantly, it's packed with fruit and approachable.

2005 Yalumba 'Mawson's' Cabernet Sauvignon $14.95

The link with explorer Douglas Mawson is fascinating as Yalumba was one of the sponsors of his 1911–14 Antarctic expeditions, underlining the fact that Yalumba is one of Australia's oldest family-owned wineries. Their Senior Red Winemaker, Peter Gambetta, is responsible for the Wrattonbully vineyard from which this wine is sourced. The 2005 vintage was a terrific one for the region so it's not surprising that the 2005 'Mawson's' Cabernet is soft, round and almost syrupy in texture – generous, velvety – crammed with fresh, clean, ripe redcurrant and cassis flavours, finishing vibrant and long. It is fantastic to see such a delicious wine from a premium area at this price! A quintessential quaffer.

 **GOOD**

2005 De Bortoli 'Deen Vat 9' Cabernet Sauvignon $10.95

This is an appealing, drink-me-now style from the Riverina that has fleshy dark berry and juicy blackcurrant flavours.

2006 Earthworks Cabernet Sauvignon $14.95

This is a second label for the Barossa Valley's Langmeil that has attractive fruity flavours, smooth texture and pleasant drinkability.

2004 Jacob's Creek 'Reserve' Cabernet Sauvignon $16.95

Although the retail price is above the cut-off, the team at Pernod Ricard has indicated that the promotional price is $13.95 – so make sure you look for that. For me, this is an interesting red as I didn't like it as much of most of the members of the tasting panel. I found its tannins too heavy and dominant. There's heaps of dark berry fruits, quality vanillin oak, lots of richness and concentration and those tannins. Plenty of people (including my wife, Elaine) love the style. Whatever, drink it with a robust, slow-cooked beef stew or a chunky sirloin accompanied by a powerful red wine jus.

2005 Penfolds 'Koonunga Hill' Cabernet Sauvignon $14.95

A reliable label in a very good vintage so it's no surprise that the 2005 Koonunga Hill Cabernet is easy to like: soft, approachable with ripe red berry flavours, silky smooth texture and a supple, gentle finish. Quaff on!

2006 Penfolds 'Rawsons Retreat' Cabernet Sauvignon $10.95

While this lacks the richness and concentration of the Koonunga Hill it has the same succulence, ripe juicy fruit and quaffability.

2005 Sandalford 'Element' Cabernet Sauvignon $12.95

Paul Boulden has managed to lift the quality of the 'Element' range – in some cases dramatically. This is an easy-drinking red sourced from around Western Australia with ripe redcurrant flavours, reasonable weight and depth, smooth texture and moderate approachable tannins.

2004 Tobacco Road Cabernet Sauvignon $12

This comes from the Victorian Alps winery, has aromatic coconutty oak, is supple, round and smooth with concentrated dark berry fruit and heaps of oak and tannin. It's a bold, robust style that will appeal to many (but not all).

2006 Yalumba 'Y Series' Cabernet Sauvignon $11.95

While it's a notch below the sublime quality of the 'Y Series' Shiraz Viognier and Shiraz, not having the same concentration of flavour, it is an impressive wine in its own right. Certainly, there's a touch of elegance – as well as pleasing blackcurrant and red cherry flavours, smooth texture and ripe balanced tannins.

▶ PRETTY GOOD

2004 Baily & Baily Cabernet Sauvignon $11.95

An easy-drinking Coonawarra style with minty dark berry flavours, silky smooth texture and fine ripe tannins. Exclusive to Woolworths.

2004 Leasingham 'Magnus' Cabernet Sauvignon $14.95

A decent quaffer from the Clare Valley that has smoky oak, red plum and blackberry flavours and a gentle tannin grip.

2006 Lindemans 'Bin 45' Cabernet Sauvignon $9.95

One of the Reliables offering decent value – as ever. This vintage is light- to medium-bodied, has good red berry flavours, smooth texture and plenty of tannins to finish.

2006 McWilliam's 'Hanwood' Cabernet Sauvignon $12

A reliable cabernet from the Riverina, fleshed out with some Coonawarra fruit which adds depth and some darker berry flavours to the wine. This is full-bodied with layers of redcurrant and blackberry flavours, chewy texture and a powerful finish.

2006 Preece Cabernet Sauvignon $14

I loved the 2005 but am less enthusiastic about this vintage of the Preece (which has lost its reference to Mitchelton): it's supple, round and easy drinking with clean redcurrant flavours and a slight grippiness to finish.

2005 Saltram 'Maker's Table' Cabernet Sauvignon $9.95

> A pleasant quaffer from Saltram and the Barossa – clean, fresh, blackcurrant and dark plum flavours, with a firm grip to finish.

2006 Zilzie Cabernet Sauvignon $14.95

> A Murray–Darling favourite that has ripe, dark cherry flavours, smooth texture, and a firm, grippy finish.

MERLOT

The general decline in the amount of red varieties produced has slowed the pace of merlot's growth – at least temporarily. Merlot rosé by 17% from 2004 to 2005 (to 144 400 tonnes) while shiraz crept up 4% (to 454 200 tonnes) and cabernet declined by 5% (to 303 600 tonnes). Merlot slipped back in 2006 – along with almost every red variety – to 131 000 tonnes. However, it had increased by more than 30% from 93 000 tonnes in 2003 and a backward historical look reminds us how little merlot was produced before 1990: 1000 tonnes were produced in 1988 and 8000 tonnes in 1996.

Merlot is much loved and much maligned. At its rare best – when it is ripe, silkily textured, in harmony with gentle oak – it can be immediately appealing and a great drink. As a varietal in Australia, too often it is thin, green, weedy, over-oaked and completely lacking in charm. Those who see wines like the latter can have some sympathy with Miles, in the film *Sideways*, and his comment 'I'm leaving if anyone orders merlot'.

While plenty of expensive merlots disappoint, there are many very drinkable merlots at the quaffing price points. In fact, it seems that when the winemakers chill out and don't try too hard – by cramming too much oak into the wine or extracting every last ounce of tannin, the result can be much more drinkable – a fun-filled, juicy red fruit bomb that is a pleasure to gulp. Don't doubt it for a second: merlot is still popular, especially in *Quaff* land.

The reliable – consistent-quality wines, year in, year out

The McWilliam's 'Hanwood' has appeared in seven out of eight editions of *Quaff*, making it the most consistent and reliable example of the variety at this price point.

Buying and Drinking Merlot – Some Tips

Balance is all

You'll see very clearly the style of merlot that I believe makes the best drink: one that doesn't have too much oak or tannins, which is not over-extractive, and one that isn't too heavy or too strong. This means that the wines need to be balanced – the fruit should match the oak treatment and the tannins. As a general rule, wines at this price point have neither the richness nor concentration to cope with a great deal of oak or massive tannins. That's why merlot is often at its best when it's least manipulated.

Different styles

Having stated a clear preference for soft, smooth, easy-drinking and fleshy merlots (especially at the *Quaff* price point), it should be said that I also admire the bigger, bolder, more robust and savoury reds, which might finish dry and tannic: wines such as the consistent Fishbone from Western Australia's Blackwood Valley and Capel Vale's 'Debut' from Geographe. These are different in style, but avoid excessive oaking and heavy tannins.

🍷 BLOODY GOOD

2005 Capel Vale 'Debut' Merlot $14.95

Winning a trophy at the Melbourne Wine Show is a fantastic achievement for a wine of this price. The rebadging of the Capel Vale range – with its entry point wines placed under the bright 'Debut' label – heralds a new beginning. So too, does the quality of the wines. The 2005 'Debut' Merlot has marvellous depth, silky-smooth dark plum and black cherry flavours with a savoury edge, arresting persistence and supple fine-grained tannins. It's a triumph of restraint and purity of fruit.

2006 Fishbone Merlot $14.95

The third vintage of this very successful second label for the Blackwood Valley winery in Western Australia's timber country shows its consistency with merlot: Good for the first two years and now 'Bloody Good'. No other winery has done as well with this difficult variety in the past few years. This is bold and full-flavoured with richness, concentration and depth of plummy fruit well-integrated with restrained cedary oak, velvety texture and supple, balanced tannins.

🍷 GOOD

2004 Logan 'Apple Tree Flat' Merlot $10

This is a straightforward fruity merlot – the best kind of merlot – that is smooth and viscous, almost velvety, with ripe, plummy fruit. Satisfying.

2005 'Preece' Merlot $14

A better merlot from Preece than usual: it's softer and fruitier and has no hard edges. There's ripe sweet redcurrant and red plum flavours, smooth texture, and a clean, balanced finish.

▶ PRETTY GOOD

2004 Lindemans 'Reserve' Merlot $12.95
This is soft, round and plummy and has a good mouthfeel.

2006 Little Penguin Merlot $10.95
Not as good as the previous vintage but soft, round and smooth with some richness and depth.

2006 McWilliam's 'Hanwood' Merlot $12
One of the Reliables, as consistent as ever: ripe redcurrant and dark berry flavours, silky smooth texture and a gentle balanced finish.

2006 Sandalford 'Element' Merlot $12.95
A pleasant, easy drinking style that is smooth and has ripe sweet redcurrant flavours.

2005 Trentham Merlot $14.50
This is soft, round and smooth with ripe, rich, concentrated flavours and gentle, fine tannins. Gulpable.

2006 Wolf Blass 'Eaglehawk' Merlot $9.95
Light-bodied but pleasant thanks to its smooth, soft texture and ripe redcurrant and plum flavours.

2006 Yellow Tail Merlot $9.95
While this lacks the depth or concentration of the previous vintage, it is smooth and approachable with attractive ripe sweet red berry flavours and a gentle grip to finish.

2006 Zilzie Merlot $15
Clean, fresh and easy to drink: it's soft with ripe sweet red berry fruit.

SHIRAZ

The hardy, vigorous shiraz grape has been an important part of Australia's viticultural history and has done well in our warm regions since the middle of the nineteenth century. It has been used to produce good-quality, fairly priced table wine; as fodder for cask and flagon wines; in cheap red blends (especially with grenache, cabernet sauvignon and mataro); and as a base wine for sparkling reds. With grenache, it has been an important source of fortified wine. However, in the 1980s shiraz was so unfashionable that the South Australian government offered incentives to grape growers to uproot their vines. Many now-priceless old vines were lost to the Vine Pull Scheme of 1985.

Today, shiraz is Australia's most popular grape variety – with 441 000 tonnes harvested in 2005 compared to 423 000 tonnes of chardonnay and 278 000 tonnes of cabernet sauvignon. Planting of shiraz increased sixfold in the 1990s and has increased by 50% since 2003. In 2006, it was still our most planted red variety – behind only chardonnay in terms of the number of hectares added to the viticultural landscape. While this huge increase in production has benefited our export drive and has kept down the price of quaffing wines, the most recent surge has resulted in wines being made from an unprecedented number of young vines. These can taste thin, lean and lacking in fruit; winemakers may attempt to disguise this with excessive oak flavour (by throwing too many coarse-tasting oak chips into the fermentation vats), or by adding too much tannin or leaving in too much residual sugar. The resulting wines are out of balance and taste awful. You have been saved from trying them.

There's no question about Aussie shiraz making great quaffing reds. Throughout the country, wineries are able to produce attractive, delightfully flavoursome shiraz with excellent texture and approachability. Most importantly, they are well priced. Especially at the moment when many Australian quaffing wines are a dollar or more cheaper than at this time last year – or in some cases, five years ago. The best wines can come from such diverse regions as the Barossa, McLaren Vale, Padthaway, Mudgee, Frankland River, Heathcote and the Adelaide Hills.

The reliable – consistent-quality wines, year in, year out

Rosemount Estate 'Diamond Label' is the only shiraz to be found in all eight editions of *Quaff.*

Buying and Drinking Shiraz – Some Tips

Drink now

If you are looking for a spicy red that is light- to medium-bodied, soft and approachable, you'll find some excellent examples under $10. These invariably come from the Riverina, Murray–Darling, Swan Hill or Riverland and can be great wines for immediate drinking.

Cellaring

More substantial, more full-bodied shiraz tends to be in the $12 to $15 range and usually contains a proportion of fruit from premium areas such as Coonawarra, Clare, Langhorne Creek or McLaren Vale or is sourced entirely from one of these regions. These wines can be drunk now but need to be served with robust or hearty meat dishes, to soften the impact of powerful tannins. They can repay even short-term cellaring (and the better your cellaring conditions, the longer you can keep the wines).

RED WINES UNDER $15

🍷 BLOODY GOOD

2006 Angove's 'Red Belly Black' Shiraz $14.95

A terrific follow-up to the impressive 2005 wine thanks, no doubt, to some Wrattonbully fruit that finds its way into the mix. It has very good depth of dark plum and black cherry flavours with a touch of complexity, is succulent and fleshy and finishes supple and long.

2005 Beresford 'Highwood' Shiraz $14

This sizeable (130 000+ case) operation based in McLaren Vale was set up in 1985 by Rob Dundon who is still in charge. There is an associated Langhorne Creek winery, Step Road (the current release 2004 Step Road Cabernet Sauvignon is a ripper). Wines from both have been featured prominently in *Quaff* over the years. In the case of Beresford, there are two budget labels – 'Highwood' and the cheaper 'Beacon Hill'. The 2005 Beresford 'Highwood' Shiraz is supple, round and fleshy with dark plum, blackberry, chocolate and anise flavours. Here the tannins were held in check, unlike too many of the wines in the tasting line up. So there's an approachability to the wine that makes it bloody good current drinking.

2004 Gramps Shiraz $15.95

This is the best of three outstanding consecutive vintages for the Gramps. Not surprisingly, it is big and powerful with pronounced American oak and layer after layer of opulent flavour. It shows briary, dark plum characters, neatly integrated with vanillin oak, fabulous velvety texture and a pleasingly satisfying finish. Drink with a robust oxtail stew or the like. Amazing value.

2005 Long Flat 'Destinations' Shiraz $14.95

Victorian-based virtual winery, Cheviot Bridge, bought the Long Flat label from Tyrrell's to speed up and increase the impact of their move into the North American market. While the Long Flat wines sell for $8.95, this new 'Destinations' range ($14.95) is more expensive yet offers very good value. The range is a rebadging of wines released in previous vintages under the Long Flat Wine Company label. They consist of varietal wines sourced from regions where they have been successful: sauvignon blanc from the Adelaide Hills, riesling from the Clare Valley, chardonnay from the Yarra, cabernet from Coonawarra and shiraz from the Barossa. This is lively, juicy and ridiculously easy drinking yet with a depth of clean, fresh, ripe plummy flavours. It's a modern fruity style with little oak influence – an ideal quaffer.

2006 Longhop Shiraz $15

The energetic Domenic Torzi makes his sublime Eden Valley wines – Torzi Matthews 'Frost Dodger' Riesling and 'Frost Dodger' Shiraz (the 2004 Shiraz is vibrant and succulent and has impressive generosity of fruit) as well as the superb Torzi Matthews Olive Oil – and works with high-school pal, Tim Freeland, on the Longhop and Old Plains labels. This is a terrific Adelaide Plains shiraz with much greater depth of flavour than you'd expect – as well as drinkability. Better on the palate than the nose, it has blackberry and vanilla bean flavours, velvety texture, plenty of oak and non-aggressive tannins. It's only available by mail order but you can buy a three pack (including delivery) for $45. That's value and service.

2005 Penfolds 'Koonunga Hill' Shiraz $15

About time! After a couple of indifferent years, Koonunga Hill is back on form. This has lush texture, is very ripe and rich with concentrated dark plum flavours.

RED WINES UNDER $15

2006 Red Knot Shiraz $14.95

One of the things that we want to see in the best quaffing wines is consistency. Really, it's what we all look for: wines that we can rely on from one vintage to the next. So I'm delighted to report that one of the most delicious reds from the 2005 vintage, Red Knot Shiraz, is terrific again in the following vintage. I did say that the 2005 was the best I'd seen under this label and I'll stand by that. But the 2006 is still 'Bloody Good' and in the same league. Red Knot is the second label of the Davey family who own and run Shingleback in the McLaren Vale. The 2006 Shiraz is succulent, even lush, with spicy ripe red berry flavours, good depth and length. It's made to be drunk while young and so is quite gluggable.

2005 Rockbare 'Mojo' Shiraz $14.95

Rockbare's Tim Burvill looked outside the McLaren Vale to source growers' fruit for his Mojo range. Hard to believe but he found some old-vine Barossa shiraz and can offer the resulting wines for less than $15. This has supple, silky-smooth texture, power, richness and concentration of dark berry fruit, pleasing succulence and neat balance.

2005 Rosemount Estate 'Diamond Label' Shiraz $15.95

This is the pick of the Rosemount new releases and bewildering good shiraz. If its retail price had been below $15, it would have featured in the shortlist for the Awards. So, if you can buy it for less than $15 (and I'm sure it'll be readily available in that price range), don't hesitate. There is layer after layer of dark plum and blackberry flavours, a smooth almost velvety texture, tremendous power and fine approachable tannins.

2006 Sticks Shiraz Viognier $13.95

This is surprisingly well priced, even for Sticks who normally pride themselves on modest prices. This is clean, fresh and bright with generous floral perfumes, ripe red berry and dark plum flavours and smooth texture with some chewiness. It's approachable now with a dish like spaghetti, meatballs and a ragu bolognese.

2004 Vintage Cellars (Barossa) Shiraz $13.95

This is a style of Barossa shiraz that will appeal to many (though not all). There's overt vanilla bean oak that is almost coconutty on the nose and palate, rich, concentrated flavour, silky texture, fair balance between the fruit and tannins with vanilla bean characters lingering on the finis.

2005 Rex Watson Shiraz $14.95

The combination of a newish label and the excellent 2005 vintage has produced a powerful, briary, dark berry flavoured red that is smooth and succulent before finishing clean and fresh.

2006 Westend 'Richland' Shiraz $10.95

One or two budget reds each year stand out from the pack as offering fantastic value. This is one such wine. It's from Bill Calabria and his team at a standout Riverina winery – and is their best red under the label since at least 2003. Bright crimson in colour, this has lively, juicy redcurrant and black plum flavours, is succulent and fleshy, almost velvety, before a clean, refreshing finish. A delicious quaffer.

2006 Yalumba 'Y Series' Shiraz $11.95

I tasted more than 100 shiraz for *Quaff 2008*, mostly in blind tastings of 28 wines. On one of these occasions, the two top performers were this wine and the Yalumba 'Y Series' Shiraz Viognier. This is deep and powerful with dense dark berry flavours, a hint of brambles, black plums; succulent and silky smooth, almost seamless (not something I'd normally say about a wine at this price). In a word, impressive. A quintessential quaffer.

RED WINES UNDER $15

⭐ 2006 Yalumba 'Y Series' Shiraz Viognier $11.95

**THE QUAFF 2008 'Fillet Steak and Chips'
RED WINE OF THE YEAR AWARD**

Fabulous! Last year's *Quaff* Wine of the Year topped a tasting of shiraz for *Quaff* and, in my view, is at least as good as last year's wine. The 2005 wine has matured nicely in the 12 months since I last saw it and is a better wine now than it was then. Expect this vintage to improve then. There's spicy liquorice and blackcurrant flavours, succulent, silky smooth texture, terrific depth and length and lingering spicy flavours. It's primal, focused, as good as it gets.

🍾 GOOD

2006 Angove's 'Nine Vines' Shiraz Viognier $14.95

There's some attractive wild berry aromas, ripe dark berry flavours, good weight, supple, smooth texture and gentle tannins.

2005 Capel Vale 'Debut' Shiraz $14.95

More evidence of a Capel Vale upheaval. This has lush, velvety texture, rich, concentrated dark berry flavours with cedary oak notes, power and a firm, slightly grippy finish.

2006 Earthworks Shiraz $14.95

Here's a bright young Barossa shiraz that has rich, concentrated redcurrant and dark plum flavours, smooth, almost velvety texture and soft ripe tannins.

2006 De Bortoli 'Wild Vine' Shiraz $8.50

This is light-bodied, bright and fruity and so is soft, easy drinking and flavoursome. Quaff on!

2005 De Bortoli 'Windy Peak' Shiraz $14.95

The De Bortoli Victorian label is consistently over-delivering. This is rich and full with dark berry flavours and an oaky edge, smooth texture, power and approachable tannins.

2006 Fishbone Shiraz $14.95

Another wine to stand out from this small Western Australian producer: pepper and spice, ripe sweet brambly flavours and gentle succulence.

2005 Gnangara Shiraz $12

The wines in this Evans & Tate range are looking better than ever this year. There's redcurrant and red cherry flavours with some earthiness, substantial tannin and a dry finish.

2004 Jacob's Creek 'Reserve' Shiraz $16.95

On promotion at $13.95, so look for that. Age has softened the wine so there's ripe, gentle plummy flavours, smooth texture and a slight grip to finish.

2006 Kirrihill 'Companions' Shiraz Viognier $14.95

There's noticeable coconut and vanilla bean characters on the nose and palate of this entry-level red from a large Clare Valley winery. As well as this, you'll find dark plum and blackberry flavour, smooth, fleshy texture and an approachable finish.

2005 Little Penguin Shiraz $10.95

While this is primarily an export label for Foster's, there's plenty for Australian consumers to love, too. There's redcurrant and red plum flavours here with a pleasant juiciness, even succulence, and noticeable but moderate tannins.

2005 Long Flat Shiraz $9.90

This may need a good swirl or decanting to aerate it, but there's plenty of rich fruit, some smooth, almost lush texture before a finish that grips gently.

2005 McWilliam's 'Hanwood' Shiraz $12

One of the great Riverina family wineries with substantial holdings around the country: and this is their most important quaffing label. The shiraz in 2005 has a depth of sweet black jubes and raspberry pastille flavours, a juicy succulence and powerful tannins that are in balance with the fruit weight.

2004 Mount Langi Ghiran 'Billi Billi' Shiraz $14.95

There are now three levels of shiraz at the Grampians winery, Mount Langi Ghiran: the flagship ($55) which in 2003 is an excellent example of cool-climate shiraz – restrained, briary, white pepper flavours, succulent and fleshy with depth and richness and ripe, fine-grained tannins; 'Cliff Edge' (about $25) from younger vines on the estate and growers' fruit, aged in French oak; and the 'Billi Billi', which is sourced from growers. Amazingly, the 'Billi Billi' fruit comes from 80 to 100-year-old bush vines. The 2004 Mount Langi Ghiran 'Billi Billi' Shiraz is a neatly balanced red that is supple, round and smooth, showing rich, concentrated redcurrant and dark plum flavours with a gentle grip to finish.

2005 Norfolk Rise Shiraz $16

This impressive Mount Benson winery is part of the Kreglinger empire, along with Tasmania's Piper's Brook. The successful 2005 vintage has produced a rich, concentrated dark berry red that is in balance with its tannins – so it's very easy to drink.

2004 Plantagenet 'Hazard Hill' Shiraz $12

I would have expected a Plantagenet shiraz at this price to have sold out by now. It's drinking easily with pleasant, smooth, red berry flavours.

2004 Richmond Grove 'Black Cat' Shiraz $13.95

This is a powerful shiraz sourced from Coonawarra and Padthaway and so represents excellent value. There's heaps of dense, dark berry fruit and fine, ripe tannins to match it. It does need a hearty oxtail stew or a similarly slow-cooked dish to enhance the experience.

2006 Willow Bridge Shiraz $15.50

The Ferguson Valley in Geographe where Willow Bridge is situated is admirably suited to sauvignon blanc, semillon and shiraz. This is vibrant and juicy with ripe raspberry and mulberry flavours and substantial tannins.

2005 Xanadu 'Dragon' Shiraz $14.95

Under the Rathbone family, Xanadu is one of Margaret River's big improvers. Chief Winemaker Glenn Goodall is crafting some excellent wines. The whites have been the quickest to turn around but the reds are showing promise. The Dragon range wines are uncomplicated quaffers that offer value. This shiraz is improving with time yet is still quite tannic: fortunately, the richness of the redcurrant and dark plum fruit is helping to soften and make the wine more appealing. Try with sausages, mash, fried onions and, of course, a green salad.

 PRETTY GOOD

2006 Angove's 'Long Row' Shiraz $9.95

This is soft, round and silky-smooth showing ripe red berry flavours and substantial yet balanced tannins.

2005 Cookoothama Shiraz $14.95

Coconutty, vanillin oak dominates yet there is some richness and concentration: a powerful, robust shiraz.

2005 Deakin Estate Shiraz $10

There's bright redcurrant and ripe plum fruit, substantial tannins and some firmness to finish.

RED WINES UNDER $15

2006 De Bortoli 'Deen Vat 8' Shiraz $10.95
>This is light-bodied and a bit lacking in concentration yet has decent red berry flavours and drinks well.

2005 Jacob's Creek Shiraz $10.95
>There's ripe sweet fruit, smooth texture and dense flavours though it's firm to finish.

2006 Leaping Lizard Shiraz $14.95
>Attractive floral perfumes, fresh garden herbs and smooth red berry flavours.

2006 Lindemans 'Bin 50' Shiraz $9.95
>A consistent performer than has fine ripe flavours and smooth easy drinkability.

2004 Redbank 'Long Paddock' Shiraz $12.95
>Sourced from the King Valley and showing spicy fruit and smooth texture.

2005 Tyrrell's 'Old Winery' Shiraz $12.95
>Ripe redcurrants lead you into a soft, round, easy-drinking shiraz with some sweetness.

2005 Vintage Cellars Shiraz Viognier $13.95
>There's plenty of dark berry and vanilla bean character here along with heaps of extraction on the finish.

2006 Yalumba 'Oxford Landing' Shiraz $7.95
>It does appear a bit oaky but has smooth, rich texture and juicy redcurrant flavours.

OTHER RED VARIETALS

Think about the reds in this chapter as including a group of grapes that have been around in Australia for some time – malbec, pinot noir, petit verdot, durif, as well as tarrango – and some classic European varieties that are beginning to be planted in significant amounts – sangiovese, tempranillo and nebbiolo. It's a pretty diverse bunch.

There is some excitement with the best of these wines. Many provide taste experiences outside the mainstream and are recommended for much the same reason as I'd advocate trying some exotic varieties that have been imported from overseas: being adventurous can be fun.

The reliables – consistent-quality wines, year in, year out

The wonderfully robust Bleasdale Malbec is one of the Reliables and has been included in every edition of *Quaff*. Labels that have consistently appeared in this chapter include De Bortoli 'Windy Peak', Trentham Estate and Zilzie.

Buying and Drinking Other Red Varietals – Some Tips

The perfect match
Thinking about what wines will go best with what foods should probably start with traditional matches. Duck and pinot noir are considered a classic pairing, although I believe that lighter bodied meats such as veal and pork also work well with pinot – especially when the dish incorporates mushrooms, which find an earthy echo in the wine. Sangiovese will go well with many Tuscan dishes and also try roast pork, pasta with tomato-based pasta dishes, or even pizza. More full-bodied reds such as malbec and petit verdot demand robust, slow-cooked meat dishes or grilled steak with hearty red-wine sauces.

Wines by the glass
Look for the opportunity to try these varieties in restaurants and cafes, especially when you can experiment by buying by the glass. When you find a variety you like, look around for a few more examples that suit your palate and add that variety to your vinous portfolio.

OTHER RED VARIETALS

🍾 BLOODY GOOD

2005 Angove's 'Stonegate' Petit Verdot $8.95

Petit verdot is a classic, late-ripening variety that is more widely planted in the irrigated areas along the Murray than in its native Bordeaux. Here, it makes delicious robust reds with powerful, mouth-coating tannins. Remarkably, they are nowhere near as popular as they deserve to be. This is bold, full-throttled, with deeply concentrated blackberry pastille flavour and substantial, though balanced, tannins: a well-priced quaffer.

2003 Bleasdale Malbec $13.50

The Langhorne Creek family winery has been one of the Reliables, with their Malbec appearing in every issue of *Quaff.* I'm surprised that we're still on the 2003 as it's drinking exceptionally well. In fact, another year has pushed it up from Good to Bloody Good. The power of the oak hasn't diminished nor the density of its fruit flavour.

2005 De Bortoli 'Deen Vat 1' Durif $10.95

The secret with durif is to tame its power and fierce tannins and to harness its concentrated flavour. De Bortoli succeeds admirably here with a gently perfumed, rich, ripe densely flavoured fruit bomb that is smoothly textured and has restrained tannins. It's a good drink.

2006 De Bortoli 'Windy Peak' Pinot Noir $14.95

Spectacular! This is a stunning effort from the team at De Bortoli in the Yarra. Sourcing and crafting a large-volume varietal pinot of this quality is some achievement. I love its soft, silky, even velvety texture, finesse and elegant, piercingly pure wild berry flavours and assured pristine finish.

2005 Trentham Estate Pinot Noir $12.50

You might not expect that anyone could make decent pinot noir in a place as warm as Mildura so this is a surprise packet. It's varietal, light-bodied, soft, round and perfumed with silky smooth texture, ripe red cherry and strawberry flavours of good intensity. A lovely drink.

 **GOOD**

2005 De Bortoli 'Deen Vat 4' Petit Verdot $10.95

Sourced from De Bortoli's Riverina operations, this is a robust red with richness, power, depth, impressive weight and marvellous drinkability.

2007 De Bortoli 'Windy Peak' Pinot Noir $14.95

This has very good varietal character, depth of flavour on the nose and palate as well as good concentration of dark cherry flavour and fine gentle tannins. It's textural and complex.

2005 De Bortoli 'Windy Peak' Sangiovese $14.95

This was reviewed last year and I'm surprised that it's still around as it's a good example of a variety that has proved difficult to produce in Australia. There's a bit more softness about this now, especially on the finish. It's still easy drinking with slightly chewy texture and a savoury edge. Gnocchi with a bolognese ragu would still be my preferred dish.

 PRETTY GOOD

2005 Capel Vale 'Debut' Pinot Noir $14.95

Sourced from Capel Vale's Pemberton vineyard, this has gentle silky texture, toasty oak and red cherry flavours and moderate balanced tannins.

2006 Coldstone Tempranillo $12

This is one of the labels of the Victorian Alps winery. It has rich brambly flavours, powerful oak and chewy texture: interesting with food, say paella with chorizo and red wine.

2006 Logan 'Weemala' Pinot Noir $14.95

This is soft, round and drinks well; has reasonable varietal character, and is silky smooth with gentle, fine tannins.

2006 Westend 'Calabria' Saint Macaire $14.95

Saint Macaire is a village on the opposite side of the river from Sauternes in Bordeaux – and it's also a grape variety. I don't know of anyone else but Bill Calabria who produces a wine from it. It's aromatically intriguing with talc, musk stick fragrances, ripe sweet fruit flavours and high acidity to finish. Different.

2006 Wyndham Estate 'Bin 333' Pinot Noir $14.95

This is a pleasant, light-bodied pinot with reasonable varietal character and good concentration of flavour.

2006 Zilzie Petit Verdot $14.95

Petit verdot does particularly well in the Murray–Darling: this is rich, ripe and powerful with dark plum and black cherry flavours and heaps of tannins.

CABERNET MERLOT BLENDS

There have been huge amounts of merlot planted in the last decade in Australia and so there are many more varietal merlots and a plethora of cabernet merlot blends stocking the shelves in retail land. The ease of pronunciation and the sweet sound of the word 'merlot' have surely helped its popularity, as has its perceived softness.

The marriage of cabernet sauvignon – with its firmer structure, occasionally hollow mid-palate and drying grip – and merlot – with its fleshy smoothness, plump mid-palate and softer, gentler finish – can produce some beautifully balanced, flavoursome reds. But the reality is that only three out of more than 44 cabernet merlots tasted for *Quaff* this year have been rated Bloody Good. Fewer than half of those tasted are reviewed in this chapter. Many of the other wines are either powerful, oaky and almost unapproachable, or skinny and tough

The reliables –
consistent-quality wines, year in, year out

This is an emerging category with no clear-cut Reliables. Most consistent have been De Bortoli, Lindemans, Rosemount Estate, Rouge Homme and Trentham Estate.

Buying and Drinking Cabernet Merlot Blends – Some Tips

The $10 price point

There tends to be a division between those wines under $10 and those which sell for between $10 and $15. The best of the former have more redcurrant, raspberry flavours while the latter tend to have darker berry fruit – often because of the addition of up to 20% of fruit from some of Australia's premium regions. Those under $10 usually come from regions along the Murray River (the Riverland, Swan Hill and Murray-Darling) and the Murrumbidgee (the Riverina). They are lighter bodied and more straightforward, but the best of them are delicious, everyday quaffers. This may be the last year that I can make this comment as many wines are moving upward in price and there's a bit of a cluster at $12. Still, my comment about the split holds for the moment.

Bottle age

A number of those cabernet merlots that have been recommended come from premium regions and have enough richness and concentration of flavour and sufficient tannin grip to improve with time in your cellar. Capel Vale, Ferngrove and Mount Trio are the wines most likely to benefit from additional bottle age. Having said that, the great thing about under-$15 wines is that they are approachable enough to drink now without having to worry about cellaring.

RED WINES UNDER $15

▶ BLOODY GOOD

2005 Capel Vale 'Debut' Cabernet Merlot $14.95

Another example of the Larry Cherubino broomstick sweeping through the Capel Vale operation with very pleasing results. This medium-bodied red blend is restrained, even fine; highlighting bright blackcurrant and red cherry flavours which persist. There's succulence which entices and balance on the finish. Classy.

2005 Ferngrove 'Symbols' Cabernet Merlot $14.95

While I've loved Ferngrove's more expensive reds and budget-priced whites, this is the first of its under-$15 reds that I've been delighted with. There's power, richness and concentration, layer after layer of ripe, fleshy, brambly, dark berry flavours. Stunningly good.

2006 Westend 'Richland' Cabernet Merlot $10.95

The affable Bill Calabria and the guys at Westend make some terrific wines from their base at Griffith on the Riverina. Often at this price point, reds can lack some grunt, or to put it into my usual sophisticated winespeak, weight and depth of flavour. There's attractive musk stick and blackberry pastille fragrances, smooth texture, dark plum and blackcurrant flavours with some floral notes. The tannins are noticeable yet ripe, quite fine, and in balance so the wine has an approachability that makes it good current drinking – though you could hold on to it for a little while

▶ GOOD

2005 Lindemans Reserve Cabernet Merlot $12.95

A Limestone Coast cab merlot that is rich, concentrated, smooth and ridiculously easy drinking. It's all the redcurrant and cassis flavours and neatly balanced tannins.

CABERNET MERLOT BLENDS

2006 McWilliam's 'Inheritance' Cabernet Merlot $7.50

A year later and this outstanding vintage of the 'Inheritance' Cab Merlot is looking as good as ever. It's is clean, fresh and lively, has bright redcurrant and cassis flavours and beautifully integrated tannins. Quaff on!

2005 Mount Trio Cabernet Merlot $14.95

I'd probably expect something more elegant from Gavin Berry and Gill Graham's family label but I wouldn't be complaining about the price of this Western Australian cab merlot or its dense dark berry and coconutty oak flavours.

2006 Vino Gusto Cabernet Merlot $5.95

I wasn't all that sure about this label but I guess that the guys from Vintage Cellars know their market. What surprised me even more is the quality of a couple of the wines – especially considering their price. Take this for example. There's quality ripe red cherry and blackcurrant flavours and silky smooth texture in this pleasant light-bodied red. Even a hint of finesse. Value. Exclusive to Vintage Cellars.

 PRETTY GOOD

2005 Cookoothama Cabernet Merlot $14.95

Vanilla bean and coconut oak aromas flow through to the palate, which is rich and concentrated; just a bit too oaky for me.

2005 Coriole 'Redstone' Cabernet Merlot $14.95

A consistent quaffer for this fine McLaren Vale producer: in 2005, it has powerful dark berry fruit with a charry oak edge and generous fleshy texture.

2006 De Bortoli 'Sacred Hill' Cabernet Merlot $6.50

More power than you'd expect from a Riverina cheapie – vibrant red berry flavours and firm tannins.

RED WINES UNDER $15

2005 Gnangara Cabernet Merlot $12
: This is a Western Australian red that is soft, round and easy to drink as rich, concentrated fruit balances firm, fine tannins.

2005 Kirrihill 'Companions' Cabernet Merlot $14.95
: An entry-level Clare Valley cabernet blend that is supple and round with ripe dark berry fruit and a charry oak edge.

2004 O'Leary Walker 'Blue Cutting Road' Cabernet Merlot $14.95
: This is one of a new entry-level range for Clare's O'Leary Walker team. It drinks well thanks to ripe redcurrant and blackberry flavours, smooth texture and a touch of finesse.

2006 Rosemount Estate 'Diamond Cellars' Cabernet Merlot $11.95
: A pleasant, easy-drinking red with redcurrant and blackberry flavours – an excellent mid-week quaffer.

2004 Rouge Homme Cabernet Merlot $14.95
: This Limestone Coast cabernet blend has a slight firmness on the finish but still drinks well with its ripe sweet blackcurrant fruit and smooth texture.

2005 Trentham Estate Cabernet Merlot $14.50
: There's a powerful tannic streak that is almost balanced by concentrated blackberry flavours and velvety texture. For those who love bold robust reds.

2006 Westend Estate 'Outback' Cabernet Merlot $7.95
: The cheapie of the Riverina's Westend Estate: musk stick aromas, sweet red berry flavours and firm, reasonably strong tannins.

GRENACHE BLENDS

Grenache has been one of Australia's most significant grape varieties because of its suitability in the making of fortifieds – until the last 30 years the most important style of wine produced here. Following the decline in the popularity of fortifieds since the 1970s, grenache was blended away into bulk and cask wines. Yet, as recently as the early 1990s, there was more grenache grown in Australia than cabernet sauvignon. Now there is about 12 times as much cabernet as grenache.

What has saved grenache has been the renewed interest in low-yielding, dry-grown old vine grenache in regions such as the Barossa and McLaren Vale and the production of premium, super-premium or ultra-premium grenache from these vineyards. The opulent, powerfully concentrated, ripe, fleshy reds have sold for high prices and helped to forge reputations for the likes of Charles Melton, Torbreck, Turkey Flat, Kaesler, Clarendon Hills, D'Arenberg and newcomers such as Kilikanoon, Teusner and Kalleske.

One of the spin-offs can be seen in the small number of deliciously vibrant quaffers that are represented in this chapter. Especially as part of a blend, grenache can make appealing, gluggable, early-drinking reds at affordable prices.

The reliables – consistent-quality wines, year in, year out

There's been a Peter Lehmann red ever-present in *Quaff*. What was originally marketed as a varietal grenache is now the Shiraz Grenache. The winery added a Grenache Shiraz Mourvedre blend to the list from the 2003 vintage. D'Arenberg 'The Stump Jump' has been in seven out of the eight editions of *Quaff*.

Buying and Drinking Grenache Blends – Some Tips

A blended red

There is a single varietal grenache in this chapter. In the past two years, there had been no varietal grenaches featured in this section – just grenache blended with reds that have an affinity with it. In its homeland, Spain, and in the south of France where it flourishes, grenache (garnacha in Spain) is most often used as part of a red blend.

Young, warm and wonderful

While there are a few exceptions – and they are not at this price point – grenache blends produced in Australia are best consumed young, when they are fresh, fleshy and flavoursome. They are so drinkable that there is no point in cellaring them.

GRENACHE BLENDS

▶ BLOODY GOOD

2006 Schild Estate Grenache Mataro Shiraz $14.95

What a superb quaffer! The Schild family has been growing grapes in the Barossa for more than 50 years and recently began to make wines under its own label. This is vibrant, fresh, spotlessly clean and beautifully balanced. There are heaps of ripe, sweet raspberry, mulberry, brambly flavours, unctuous softness, velvety texture and a gentle delicious finish. Drink young.

▶ GOOD

2006 Mount Hurtle Grenache Shiraz Mourvedre $8.95

Geoff Merrill knows grenache and grenache blends well but I'm amazed that he can make a wine like this at such a price. It's supple, almost fleshy, has spice and dark plum flavours with a hint of raspberries and brambles.

▶ PRETTY GOOD

2006 D'Arenberg 'The Stump Jump' Grenache Shiraz Mourvedre $11.95

While this doesn't match up to last year's brilliant wine, it's a most drinkable red. There's attractive red berry flavours and restrained oak and tannins.

2005 Bethany Grenache $15.90

This Barossa varietal from the Schrapel family near the hamlet of Bethany is supple, round and mouth-filling with good richness and concentration, but is possibly a bit tough to finish.

2006 Peter Lehmann Barossa Shiraz Grenache $12.50

A supple, round Barossa blend that is rich and concentrated with earthy gravelly complexity. Perfect with a plate of German meats from the region.

RED WINES UNDER $15

2005 Peter Lehmann GSM $14.95

This Grenache Shiraz Mourvedre blend from the Barossa is light bodied with some savoury characters and a gentle dry finish.

2006 Wolf Blass 'Red Label' Shiraz Grenache $13.95

This is a rich, concentrated red blend with sweet dark berry flavours and substantial tannins. Needs food: a dish such as grilled lamb cutlets with three veg would be ideal.

SHIRAZ CABERNET BLENDS

Shiraz cabernet blends are a uniquely Australian red wine style and include some of our great wines: Penfolds 'Bin 389', Yalumba 'Signature', Majella 'Mallaea' and McWilliam's '1877'. All but four Penfolds Granges have a small amount of cabernet to go with its shiraz – although it might be stretching the point to call Grange a shiraz cabernet blend. The blend is considered unfashionable because it combines a grape from the French region of Bordeaux (cabernet sauvignon) with one from the Rhone Valley (shiraz). The French can't blend these varieties legally in most parts of the country – although rumour suggests that it was common practice in Bordeaux in earlier times. Anyway, the blend works well in Australia, especially with quaffing wines such as those reviewed here.

Two excellent shiraz cabernets are reviewed in the Great-Value Wines over $15 chapter – the Penley Estate 'Condor' Shiraz Cabernet and 'The Musician' Cabernet Shiraz from Majella, both from Coonawarra.

Buying and Drinking Shiraz Cabernet Blends – A Tip

Cellaring potential

There are two styles of shiraz cabernet reviewed in this chapter: the soft, easy-drinking styles like the 2006 Hardys 'Nottage Hill' Cabernet Shiraz and the 2004 Leasingham 'Circa 1893' Shiraz Cabernet and those richer, more concentrated wines with firm finishes or substantial tannins such as the 2006 Anvers 'Brabo' or the two Coonawarra reds mentioned on the previous page, 'Condor' and 'The Musician'. The latter are more likely to improve with short-term cellaring. A short period in the coolest, darkest part of your house could well see you rewarded with wines that have been softened and are more ready to drink. If you haven't done this before, be sure to monitor any wines you put down by drinking one from time to time.

SHIRAZ CABERNET BLENDS

▄▶ BLOODY GOOD

2004 Leasingham 'Circa 1893' Shiraz Cabernet $9
Another excellent quaffer in this new budget range from Hardys in the Clare Valley: super smooth, rich, ripe and satisfying.

▄▶ GOOD

2006 Banrock Station Shiraz Cabernet $9.50
Sourced from Hardys Riverland vineyards, which are worth a visit to see the extensive wetlands that the winery has worked to rehabilitate. This has some beguiling briary flavours, is velvety smooth and satisfying.

2006 Hardys 'Nottage Hill' Cabernet Shiraz $10.50
There's some vanilla bean oak character and dark berry flavours, smooth succulence and softness, which make it very easy drinking.

2006 Lindemans 'Bin 55' Shiraz Cabernet $9.95
This is a consistent performer in this cheaper price bracket. It is a straightforward red with ripe red berry flavours, smooth texture and a gentle finish.

2006 Rosemount 'Diamond Cellars' Shiraz Cabernet $11.95
This is a good example of the perceptible lift in the quality of the Rosemount wines submitted for *Quaff*. There's heaps of sweet red cherry and redcurrant flavours, smooth almost silky texture and a gentle, even finish.

▄▶ PRETTY GOOD

2006 Anvers 'Brabo' Cabernet Shiraz $12
I preferred the previous vintage to this as it had the depth of flavour to match its powerful tannins. This has attractive texture and decent flavours but pretty heavy tannins.

RED WINES UNDER $15

2004 Bleasdale Shiraz Cabernet $14.95
There's plenty of ripe dark berry flavours and smooth drinkability, although some may find the oak firm.

2006 Gemtree 'Tadpole' Shiraz Cabernet $14.95
Here is an oaky McLaren Vale shiraz cabernet blend that is soft and smooth with ripe red berry and dark plum flavours.

2006 Lindemans 'Cawarra' Shiraz Cabernet $7.95
A reliable light-bodied cheapie from the Lindemans team at Karadoc in the Murray–Darling. It has good texture, decent flavours and good weight.

2006 Stony Peak Shiraz Cabernet $6.95
There's heaps of ripe sweet fruit in this pleasant medium-bodied red.

2005 Trentham Estate 'Murphy's Lore' Shiraz Cabernet $10
Great pun! Deep dark berry flavours, smooth, succulent and easy to quaff.

2006 Yalumba 'Oxford Landing' Cabernet Shiraz $7.95
From Yalumba's large Riverland vineyard comes this smooth red with depth of flavour and drinkability.

OTHER RED BLENDS

Most of the 'other red blends' are bin ends – whatever is left over at the end of vintage – and these are only occasionally successful. Others are carefully blended to produce a style which the winemaker believes will appeal to consumers. Good examples of the latter are the 'Sero' red blends of De Bortoli Chief Winemaker, Steve Webber, whose experimentation is resulting in some of the most exciting wines that I've seen in the past few years. Some winemakers have succeeded in finding a style which suits their region and are consistently producing excellent quaffing wines – albeit with unusual blends. Brown Brothers have hit the mark with their Dolcetto Syrah selling in huge volumes, no doubt massively helped by its large dose of residual sugar. While I'm usually not wild about the wine because I find it too sweet, it's particularly well made this year.

The best of the 'other red blends' tend to have deep dark berry flavours, smooth texture and soft, fine, ripe, restrained tannins and show balance between their fruit and the oak treatment they receive. Obviously, the key to this is the amount and quality of oak used in their production. As a general rule with these wines, when the oak is held back, the fruit shines.

Consumers are preferring straight varietals (especially shiraz and merlot) and these are currently easier to sell than blends. A look at this chapter suggests that because red blends are unfashionable, they can be bargains.

The reliable – consistent-quality wines, year in, year out

Peter Lehmann's 'Clancy's' has been in seven out of the eight editions of *Quaff* and is the only wine featured in this chapter with such an extensive record for consistency.

Buying and Drinking Other Red Blends – Some Tips

Labelling blends

By Australian law, wine may be labelled a straight varietal if it contains 85% or more of that grape variety. If a blend has more than 15% of another variety (or varieties), it (or they) must be named. For example, a wine that is 60% cabernet sauvignon, 30% merlot, 10% petit verdot may be labelled cabernet merlot – or cabernet merlot petit verdot. The order in which the grape varieties appear on a label indicates which variety makes the largest contribution to the blend. So a shiraz merlot cabernet will be mostly shiraz, with the smallest part of the blend being cabernet.

Drink now

These are reds made for early consumption. You'll notice that most of those reviewed are from the 2006 and 2005 vintages. They'll still be drinking well in a year or two but generally won't be improved by cellaring. Many have a slight tannic grip on the finish. Consume these with a slow-cooked lamb roast, a hearty beef casserole or some spicy sausages and they'll slip down with the greatest of ease.

▶ BLOODY GOOD

2005 Coriole 'Contour 4' Sangiovese Shiraz $14.95

Coriole has been making sangiovese since the early 1980s and so it know more about the variety than anyone. This is a fabulous red blend: restrained especially with its use of oak; some dark berry fruit characters balanced by delicious savouriness; tannins balanced by fruit weight; finishing long and dry.

2006 Water Wheel 'Memsie' Shiraz Cabernet Malbec $12

This is a wonderful red blend from Bendigo: brooding, briary flavours, smooth almost silky with approachable, ripe earthy tannins and delicious approachability.

2005 Zonte's Footstep Cabernet Malbec $14.45

The previous vintage was the *Quaff* Wine of the Year two years ago, and this is a great follow-up. It has dense, dark plum and blackberry flavours and is juicy and pleasantly smooth. Its tannins are formidable yet pretty much matched by weight of the fruit. Drinks well and should improve with short-term cellaring.

▶ GOOD

2005 De Bortoli 'Sero' Syrah Tempranillo $13.95

Not squeaky clean but lovable for all that. My suggestion is that you decant the wine before serving. Its strengths are its savouriness, its fascinating chewy texture, and its carefully managed tannins.

RED WINES UNDER $15

2004 Peter Lehmann 'Clancy's' Shiraz Cabernet Merlot $13

From the excellent 2004 vintage in the Barossa, this is a robust red blend with heaps of dense ripe fruit, some vanilla bean oak, and plenty of natural extraction to give it a pleasant grip as it finishes. Not everyone's drink of choice but brilliant at the barbecue.

▶ PRETTY GOOD

2005 Chalk Hill 'Sidetrack' Shiraz Cabernet Sauvignon Grenache $15

A McLaren Vale red with dark berry flavour, smooth texture and restrained tannins.

2006 Jacob's Creek 'Three Vines' Shiraz Cabernet Tempranillo $14.95

This is one of a new range for Jacob's Creek and I'm delighted to see that. It is medium-bodied, has good depth of dark plum and blackcurrant flavours and heavy, though manageable, tannins.

2005 McWilliam's 'Inheritance' Shiraz Merlot $7.50

This has softened in the past 12 months and is smoother and shows more attractive red cherry and redcurrant flavours, and is more quaffable.

The honey wind blows
Sweet wines under $15

SWEET WINES UNDER $15

There are three sections to this short chapter: 'sweet wines' – the fresher, lighter styles made from late-harvest aromatic grapes, such as muscat, verdelho, riesling and chenin; 'sweet reds'; and 'very sweet' wines – the lush dessert wines (or 'stickies'), which are made from much riper, more sugary, shrivelled grapes. Usually, the latter are made from semillon or riesling although the hybrid grape, taminga, makes the occasional noteworthy sticky. Generally, the grapes for these have been infected with 'noble rot' (*Botrytis cinerea*) – I'm suggesting in the title of this chapter that this can happen as a result of a 'honey wind blowing'. The noble rot speeds up the shrivelling and concentrates the grape sugars. This has the effect of significantly sweetening and concentrating the wines and contributes a rich apricot and marmalade flavour to them. Stickies are expensive to produce, which is why so few are featured here: the best are wonderful bargains. There are a couple of very good stickies, too, reviewed in the Great-Value Wines over $15 chapter. The dramatic leap in popularity of the lightly fizzy moscatos means that the Sweet Sparkling chapter has been significantly expanded.

The reliables –
consistent-quality wines, year in, year out

Once again, Brown Brothers has shown that it's the most consistent producer of Australian sweet wines under $15. Its classic sweetie, Brown Brothers Lexia, has appeared in each edition of

Quaff, until this year labelled 'Spatlese Lexia'; while the Orange Muscat & Flora and the sweet red, Dolcetto Syrah, are represented here again. The Brown Brothers Moscato (reviewed in Sweet Sparkling Wines on page 45) has made seven of the eight editions and was our first Wine of the Year. Following at least some of the way in its footsteps, a brand-new fizz, the first vintage of the sweet sparkling 2007 Brown Brothers 'Zibibbo', has won the *Quaff 2008* Sparkling Wine of the Year.

Buying and Drinking Sweet Wines – Some Tips

Drink young
Fruitiness and sweetness go hand in hand and so the best time to drink these sweet wines is while they are young, vibrant and fruity – at the stage when their primary flavours are at their peak. Drink slightly chilled and enjoy.

Matching sweet wines with food
How do you decide what dessert you will serve with these sweet wines? It depends entirely on how light or heavy the wine is. The simple rule is that the lighter and less sweet the wine is, the lighter and less sweet the dessert should be. Conversely, the heavier and sweeter the wine, the sweeter the dessert should be.

So with the sweet wines, try fruit salad, pavlova or fruit-based soufflés, and with the very sweet wines, heavier desserts such as crème brûlée, bread and butter pudding, or sticky date pudding.

All you need is a half bottle
One of the ways in which you can tell the difference between sweet and very sweet wines is that the latter is invariably sold in half bottles. On most occasions, a half bottle of dessert wine will be enough for a dinner party. It is sweeter and richer than a full bottle of table wine or even sweet wine. And at the time of the meal when we serve stickies, our appetites are beginning to flag.

Sweet Wines

◗ BLOODY GOOD

2007 Brown Brothers Lexia $13.50

There's those distinctive grapey aromas to welcome you to this refreshingly sweet white that does so well for Brown Brothers. It's full-flavoured, sweet to very sweet, soft and silky, with a crisp, clean finish. For those with a sweet tooth – but none the less impressive for that.

2007 Fishbone 'Sweetlips' Late Harvest Verdelho $14.95

Fishbone is the highly successful second label for the Blackwood Valley winery in Western Australia. They certainly hit my sweet tooth here with a very sweet white that has floral aromas, juicy tropical fruit and honey flavours, and reasonably crisp cleansing acidity. Some may find it too sweet, but just as many will love it.

◗ PRETTY GOOD

Sweet Angelina $11.95

The All Saints team have pulled out all stops on the marketing of this wine and I would expect it will be a big success for them. Its sweet flavours are attractive, even enticing, and it will appeal to all who love their wines sweet and seductive.

Sweet Reds

▶ GOOD

2007 Brown Brothers Dolcetto Syrah $15.90

This is a huge seller for Brown Brothers and it fills a niche that they've carved out for themselves. Good on them, I say. I have often found it way too sweet but this vintage appears to have better acidity and so I don't find it cloying. It has wild berry aromas, a touch of spritz, sweet redcurrant and fresh grape juice flavours and a pleasant sweet finish. Still for the sweet teeth among us.

▶ PRETTY GOOD

2006 Trentham 'Murphy's Lore' Autumn Red $10

This is a sweet fruit bomb with ripe grapey characters (reminiscent of Red Globe table grapes), a pleasing juiciness and a soft sweet finish.

2006 Watershed 'Shades' Sweet Margaret $13.95

This doesn't have distinct Margaret River fruit flavours, but it does have a pleasant sweetness that will appeal to many.

Very Sweet Wines

▶ BLOODY GOOD

2005 De Bortoli 'Deen Vat 5' Botrytis Semillon (375 ml) $10.95

This is unquestionably the best dessert wine in Australia under $15. I guess with the huge success that De Bortoli have enjoyed since their first vintage of Australia's greatest sticky, Noble One, in 1982, no one should be surprised by the quality of a quaffer like this. That experience has been put to great use in growing and making this stunner, which shows sweet ripe peaches and creamy, honey and apricot flavours with a hint of marmalade. It is intense, impeccably balanced with wonderful mid-palate sweetness in harmony with fresh, cleansing acidity, giving a sensation of dryness to finish.

▶ GOOD

2006 Brown Brothers Orange Muscat & Flora (375 ml) $9.90

This is fresh, sweet and light-bodied with some attractive aromatics and pleasing cleansing acidity.

2003 Trentham Estate Noble Taminga (375 ml) $12.50

Following in the footsteps of the awesomely good 2002 means that we can expect this sticky to age beautifully too. Certainly, it's in great shape for a four-year-old sweetie from the Murray–Darling. There are heaps of lush sweet honey, apricot, grapefruit and marmalade characters, as well as good depth of flavour before a finish that is very sweet but not cloying.

2005 Vintage Cellars Botrytis Semillon (375 ml) $9.95

This own-label sticky from Vintage Cellars is quite restrained on the nose but tastes delicious. It has lush, sweet apricot and honey characters, good concentration of flavour and lime and lemon to cleanse the palate.

Unfashionable but still great
Aussie fortifieds under $15

AUSSIE FORTIFIEDS UNDER $15

I've been saying for a while that I've felt that the world of Australian fortified wines under $15 is not the glittering panoply of bargains it once was. However, you can still find plenty of quality wines at bedrock prices in this chapter. The best of them are world class – you won't find better fortifieds anywhere at comparable prices.

The disappointing news is that production of fortifieds continues to decline – down by 12.7 ml or 37.3% since 2004/2005. The winemakers at Rutherglen were quick to inform me on my visit there in March that sales of bottled fortifieds are up and it's only cask fortifieds that are in decline. At present, fortifieds only make up about 5% of domestic sales.

> **THE QUAFF 2008 'Any Port In a Storm'**
> **FORTIFIED WINE OF THE YEAR AWARD**
>
> On the shortlist for this award are:
> **De Bortoli Show Liqueur Muscat**
> **Morris 'Black Label' Liqueur Muscat**
> **Penfolds 'Club Reserve' Aged Tawny**
> **Seppelt 'DP 30' Trafford Tawny**
>
> The six-times champ, Penfolds 'Club Reserve' Aged Tawny, is still a formidable opponent but would need to be at his peak to defeat this impressive bunch of contenders. There's little to split the other three world-class fortifieds. I've given the nod and the *Quaff 2008* 'Any Port In a Storm' Fortified Wine of the Year to the Morris 'Black Label' Liqueur Muscat for its finesse and elegance; rare indeed in a wine at this price point.

The reliables – consistent-quality wines, year in, year out

The only two fortified wines to have appeared in every edition of *Quaff* are the two Penfolds gems: the 'Club' Tawny and the 'Club Reserve' Aged Tawny. Between them – and under slightly different names (Penfolds 'Club' Port and Penfolds 'Reserve Bin 421') – they have won most of our fortified awards. The 'Club Reserve' Aged Tawny has never been rated below Bloody Good, an outstanding achievement. The big improver in this section in the past year or so has been Angove's. There were signs last year of a turnaround but this year the improvement has been dramatic.

Buying and Drinking Fortified Wines – Some Tips

Unfashionable therefore cheap

Tougher drink-driving laws and great consciousness of drinking in moderation are partly responsible for fortified wines become unfashionable. This has meant that many of the wines in this chapter are available at bargain-basement prices. It has also meant that some wine lovers are paying more for fortifieds but drinking less of them.

Plan your dinner party to include fortifieds

One of the reasons for fortifieds losing their appeal is that appetites often wane before we reach the stage of the meal where they come into their own. Plan to drink a freshly opened, slightly chilled dry sherry as an aperitif – with either freshly shucked oysters or lightly grilled prawns. For dessert, serve an opulent muscat with a paneforte-style cake (such as New Norcia Nut Cake) or a flourless chocolate cake with an intense tawny and a short black.

Port

 **BLOODY GOOD**

Angove's 'Bookmark' Tawny Port $5.50

This label has improved so much in recent times that I can hardly believe it when its identity is revealed in a blind tasting like this. Perhaps Angove's hasn't realised this tawny's quality or don't think the company can get more for it considering its humble Riverland origins. These are the only explanations I can offer for its bargain-basement price. It's unctuous, concentrated and ripe with malt, molasses and liquorice flavours, lushly texture with impressive depth and a lively fresh finish.

Morris 'Black Label' Old Tawny Port $10.95

David Morris is a genius when it comes to blending fortifieds and is a finalist in *Gourmet Traveller Wine*'s Winemaker of the Year Awards, the first fortified winemaker to be so honoured. This has raisiny characters with a hint of prunes, is soft, round and sweet with lush texture and sweet lingering flavours.

Penfolds 'Club Reserve' Aged Tawny $12.95

Remarkable consistent and still superb after all these years. This has toffee and treacle aromas, is soft, round and silky smooth, rich with concentrated toffee, treacle and honey flavours and a pleasing gentle finish. I'm not sure that it has the depth of some years but it's still brilliant value.

Seppelt 'DP 30' Trafford Tawny $13.45

This was rated Bloody Good last year and I believe it's tasting better in 2007: lifted rancio and spirity character on the nose, intense butterscotch, honey and nut flavours that are opulent and ultra-concentrated yet with impressive finesse before a neatly balanced finish that lingers.

Taminick Cellars Gold Port $15

Booth's Taminick have been at their Glenrowan vineyard and winery for a hundred years. They have vines still in production that were planted in 1919. This is a quaffer's paradise as all the wines available from their cellar door are $16 or less with the exception of the Centenary Port ($55) which celebrates their 100-year history. The trebbiano for this port was planted in 1919 and some parcels in this solera date back to 1992. This is fresh, lively and sweet with rich and intense flavours that have a rancio edge and a delightful tanginess. Mainly cellar door.

Taminick Cellars Liqueur Muscat $14

This is gently aromatic, has ripe raisiny flavours that are long, deep and full; wonderfully lush texture and a lavish raisiny finish.

 **GOOD**

2005 Angove's Fortified Shiraz $14.95

This is very much in the Aussie vintage port style – ripe, dark plum and liquorice flavours that are rich, concentrated and sweet, a lush texture, and some firm tannins to finish.

McWilliam's 'Hanwood' Classic Tawny $11.95

This is soft, round and easy drinking with some treacle flavours and hints of rancio.

🍾 PRETTY GOOD

De Bortoli 8 Year Old Tawny Port $14.95

    This is soft, round, gentle and very sweet.

Penfolds 'Club' Tawny $9.95

    This is not the superstar it usually is but it's a decent lush, ripe fortified that is a bit sweeter than I would want it to be.

Wolf Blass 'Red Label' Tawny Port $11

    This has attractive silky texture and is a pleasant sweet fortified.

Sherry

▄▄ BLOODY GOOD

Angove's 'Bookmark' Dry Sherry $4.95

While my bottle needed a bit of a swirl when it was opened, I thought that this was an impressive dry sherry – at any everyday price: it's fine, delicate, subtle and dry.

▄▄ GOOD

Angove's 'Bookmark' Cream Sherry $4.95

This is delicate, almost floral, with spicy notes before a palate that is fresh and sweet before a bright finish that cleanses and so avoids the possibility of it becoming cloying.

Angove's 'Bookmark' Medium Sherry $4.95

Another surprise packet from Angove's; this is soft, gentle, viscous and sweet yet with a dryish finish.

▄▄ PRETTY GOOD

Angove's 'Bookmark' Sweet Sherry $4.95

Fresh and gentle rancio character, deeply flavoured, viscous with some weight and a cleansing finish that prevents the sweetness from cloying.

All Saints 'The Keep' Golden Cream Sherry $13

This is a very attractive fortified that is clean, fresh and viscous, has spice, malt and honey flavours, substantial sweetness without being cloying.

Muscat and Tokay

🍾 BLOODY GOOD

De Bortoli Show Liqueur Muscat $14.95

This is stunningly good: a Riverina fortified that at this price point matches it with the best of Rutherglen. It's dense, deep and powerful with raisin, treacle and golden syrup flavours, weight, and smooth, velvety texture, before a finish that shows the spirit in impeccable balance.

Chambers Muscadelle (Tokay) $14.95

This is exactly what quaffing is all about! Bill and Stephen Chambers make some of the country's finest fortifieds – including arguably its finest, the sublime Chambers Rare Muscadelle ($250) with a tiny portion going back to the nineteenth century. Like the great muscats and tokays (muscadelles) of Rutherglen, it is deeply flavoured, profound and opulent beyond belief. At the other end of the scale is this blisteringly good everyday charmer: it has a lightness of touch that tempts you to try a glass as a nightcap. It has a perfect golden colour, is fine and sweet with honeycomb flavours, a freshness and vibrance combined with a persistence and depth of flavour yet with amazing finesse. When I tried it, it wasn't perfect on the nose, just needed some swirling to open it up – but I loved the wine. It's available at cellar door, Dan Murphy's and probably elsewhere. Quaff on!

⭐ Morris 'Black Label' Liqueur Muscat $11.95

THE QUAFF 2008 'Any Port In a Storm'
FORTIFIED WINE OF THE YEAR AWARD

This is the third year in a row that I've said 'You won't find a better Rutherglen muscat for less than $15'.

David Morris continues to craft substantial volumes of this beguiling fortified. It has ripe raisiny aromas, is rich, sweet and lush with butterscotch, malt and raisin flavours. While it's rich and concentrated, it's also light and bright and finishes gentle with an attractive sweet raisiny character that lingers.

Seppelt 'DP 37' Tokay $16.95

This opulent tokay shows malt, butterscotch and treacle flavours, silky smooth even lush texture, good depth and length. Buy when the wine merchant is offering a 20% discount to drag the price below $15.

 **GOOD**

Seppelt 'DP 33' Muscat $16.95

This has concentrated butterscotch and malt flavours, balanced sweetness and good length.

PS

Angove's 'Bookmark' Marsala $4.95

I've much more impressed with this than ever before. It has seductive caramel and dark butterscotch flavours, is very sweet, luscious with a touch of honey and spice and has an attractive refreshing finish.

Maxwell Liqueur Mead (375 ml) $19

As ever, the pick of their three products: softer, sweeter and more viscous with honey, nutmeg and cloves enlivening the finish. It is more unctuous than before and shows better use of spirit.

Maxwell Spiced Mead $12

I also liked the Spiced Mead more than usual: it has spicy, honey characters is sweet and lively with balanced spirit to finish.

The foreign legion

Imported wines under $20

IMPORTED WINES UNDER $20

The big news for lovers of *Quaff* this year has been the bold moves made into the budget-priced area by the large chains Vintage Cellars and Dan Murphys. Negociants, too, and Pernod Ricard are better represented than ever before. In addition to a reasonable range from France and Italy, there are wines from Spain, South Africa and Chile at a wide range of price points.

There's something there for everybody – and a few screaming bargains to be had for canny lovers or followers of *Quaff*. New Zealand continues to be well represented in this chapter. Although most Kiwi wines tend to be priced above $20 a bottle, the large companies do have some excellent wines within the *Quaff* range. Once again, there is a fascinating range of rosés and more white and red table wines than before.

Previously, I've justified the $20 price point for this chapter by explaining that there is a great deal available between $15 and $20 from overseas wineries and only a limited amount under $15, so the $20 price point works better for these wines. This still holds except for some bargain-basement priced wines from the large chains.

For contact details of each importer, refer to the section 'Finding the Wines' on page 217.

THE QUAFF 2008 'A Foreign Affair'
EXOTIC WHITE WINE OF THE YEAR AWARD

On the shortlist for this award are:
2006 A mano Fiano Greco
2007 Giesen Sauvignon Blanc
2006 Telmo Rodriguez 'Basa' Verdejo

The Telmo Rodriguez 'Basa' Verdejo is a beautiful crafted white quite different from what we are used to but familiar in many ways to the local taste, while the Fiano Greco of A mano is so very different from our local wines that it offers Australians something to challenge and delight them. Both are immeasurably improved by food. The 2007 Giesen Sauvignon Blanc is very primal and an excellent expression of the hugely popular Marlborough sauvignon style, and so well-priced, that it's the *Quaff 2008* White Wine of the Year.

THE QUAFF 2008 'Another Foreign Affair'
EXOTIC RED WINE OF THE YEAR AWARD

On the shortlist for this award are:
2005 Clos Petit Bellane Cotes du Rhone
2005 Portone Valpolicella
2006 Torres 'De Casta' Rosado

The Torres Rosado is an excellent expression of a bright yet dry rosé style and worth trying because it is dramatically different from Australian rosés. The Clos Petit Bellane is an excellent introduction to the wines from the South of France – a well-made red in a style very different from what is possible in this country. The winner of the *Quaff 2008* Exotic Red Wine of the Year is the 2005 Portone Valpolicella for its sheer drinkability and value for money, as well as being a terrific introduction to a style that's not very well-known here – but deserves to be.

The reliables – consistent-quality wines, year in, year out

Of the reliables which have featured in earlier editions of *Quaff*, only Montana and Stoneleigh from New Zealand are featured this year. Here's hoping that some of the wines represented here will become regulars.

> ### Buying and Drinking Imported Wines – Some Tips
>
> **Expanding horizons**
>
> There can't be many readers of this book who don't regularly eat in restaurants or cafes that feature a range of different cuisines – Italian, Greek, French, Chinese, Thai, Vietnamese ... And I'll bet that the majority of us cook dishes from lots of different countries. We all love something different, a new taste experience, something to tantalise. Trying imported wines is a bit like that, broadening one's horizons, learning a bit more about the infinite possibilities that wine offers. One of the things that I love when I'm overseas is trying the local wines. Being able to enjoy them when I'm back in Australia helps rekindle those memories – as well as providing an opportunity for me to try something different.
>
> **Wine without food - not in Europe**
>
> Most of the wines from countries such as France, Italy and Spain are just made to go with food. In these places, grapes have been grown for hundreds of years and a local cuisine has grown up alongside the region's wines. They can sometimes look pretty ordinary when tasted by themselves, but are transformed with food. You might also like to try appropriate food and wine from the same country: a French Provencale stew with a hearty red from the Minervois; a bone dry rosé from the Cotes du Rhones with a salmon fillet; your perfect spaghetti bolognese with a rustic nero d'avola.

Imported Sparkling

 **GOOD**

Alasia Moscato d'Asti $19.80

From Asti in Piedmont hails this delightfully aromatic moscato that is fresh, vibrant and sweet with pleasantly cleansing acidity. Imported by Negociants.

Freixenet 'Cordon Negro' Cava $14

The world's best-selling sparkling wine (pronounced 'fresh-annette') hails from the Penedes region just south of Barcelona. It is bottle fermented using the traditional method and has restrained yeasty aromas, is fresh, clean, bold and powerful. It's a lively dry style that is well-priced. Distributed by Bacardi Lion.

Riccadonna Asti $16.95

Riccadonna, which is based in the province of Asti in Piedmont, is one of the three largest producers of sparkling wines (spumante) in Italy, yet the quality is consistently good. This is made from moscato bianco (white muscat) and is light and bright with intense sweet grapey flavours and vibrant cleansing acidity that prevents the bubbly appearing too sweet. Imported by Fosters.

Segura Viudas Brut Reserva Cava $14

Straightforward can be impressive as with this bold, zesty cava that is clean and fresh with appley flavours and lively zippy acidity. Distributed by Bacardi Lion.

RED WINES UNDER $15

▶ PRETTY GOOD

Freixenet Brut Rosé $14

    This cava has a light pink colour, is lively, fresh, clean and uncomplicated, has creamy texture and a pleasantly dry finish. Distributed by Bacardi Lion.

Lindauer Brut $15.95

    There's some distinctive yeasty bready complexity on this lively bubbly that finishes dry and zesty. Imported by Pernod Ricard.

Lindauer Special Reserve $17.95

    There's a hint of pink in this sparkling rosé that is soft and round with bright redcurrant flavours, some yeasty characters and a lively zippy finish. Imported by Pernod Ricard.

Imported Whites

🍾 BLOODY GOOD

2006 A mano Fiano Greco $19.95
> This is a blend of two southern Italian dry white varieties, fiano and greco di tufo, that is vibrant, crisp and clean with savoury flavours and a pleasing dry finish that lingers. Imported by Trembath & Taylor.

2006 Framingham Sauvignon Blanc $19.95
> If you enjoy Kiwi sauvignon, then you'll love the 2006 Framingham. It's pretty much quintessential Marlborough sauvignon blanc – with a more modest price tag than some. The flavours run the full gamut from green pea and fresh herbs to tropical fruit – gooseberry, lychee, guava – with a complexing minerally edge. Memorably, they linger. This is tight, fine and refreshing with vibrant, taut acidity – almost spine-tingling. Imported by Pernod Ricard.

⭐ 2007 Giesen Sauvignon Blanc $19.50
> THE QUAFF 2008 'A Foreign Affair'
> EXOTIC WHITE WINE OF THE YEAR AWARD
> Not surprisingly given the quality of the 2007, this is one of the most popular and widely available of the Marlborough sauvignons. It's clean and fresh with intense gooseberry and lychee flavours, superb varietal character before a crisp, bracing finish which features passionfruit that lingers. Imported by Negociants.

2005 Hugel 'Gentil' $20.70
> Made by one of Alsace's largest producers, this is an unusual blend of gewürztraminer, pinot gris, riesling, muscat and sylvaner that, in its best years, is deliciously refreshing. In 2005, it has wonderful floral

aromatics and some spicy, rose petal notes, is soft, round and savoury in the mid-palate, and finishes long, dry, crisp, fresh and harmonious. Try with linguine in a creamy mushroom sauce. Imported by Negociants.

2006 Montana Sauvignon Blanc $19.50

I know that Montana makes 700 000 cases of this - on the way to 900 000 - but their technical skill, rigour, attention to detail and careful sourcing of fruit enables them to produce a quality wine at a decent price. This has ripe passionfruit, guava and gooseberry flavours, intensity in the mid-palate before its cleansing zesty acidity produces a finish that refreshes. Imported by Pernod Ricard.

2007 Mount Riley Sauvignon Blanc $16.95

The Buchanan family are doing extraordinarily well with this decently priced Marlborough sauvignon. The previous vintage blitzed the judges at the Perth Show and this is close to that in quality terms. It is gently aromatic, juicy and vibrant with restrained yet pure fruit flavours – tropical notes, gooseberries and passionfruit – before a crisp, clean finish. Imported by Angove's.

2006 Telmo Rodriguez 'Basa' Verdejo $22.80

The Spanish Acquisition bring some superb Spanish (and now Portuguese) wines into the country at all price points and the surf-loving Telmo Rodriguez is one of their superstars. This is from Rueda – not far from Ribera del Duero in central Spain to the north-west of Madrid – one of the country's best white wine areas. It is gently aromatic, subtle, delicate, with fresh and pristine savoury flavours and some of the tropical notes that we'd expect from verdelho. It is tightly structured, fine and finishes with taut, quartzy minerality. Imported by Spanish Acquisition.

2006 Torres 'Vina Esmeralda' $15.70

The 2003 vintage was the *Quaff* Imported White Wine of the Year in 2006. It is sourced from the mountainous regions of the Upper Renedes to the south of Barcelona and is made from the aromatic moscatel and gewürztraminer. Headily aromatic with delightful fragrances of fresh grapes, rose petals and Turkish delight, a soft, round mouthfeel before a surprisingly cleansing dry finish that lingers. Imported by Negociants.

 **GOOD**

2006 Braided River Sauvignon Blanc $18.95

This is a good example of why Marlborough sauvignon is such a good drink. It's restrained, clean, fresh and plump, with ripe sweet fruit and some cool tropical characters. There's no distinctive flavours but it's easy to enjoy. Imported by Cheviot Bridge.

2004 Portone Soave $7.95

Soaves are refreshing, unoaked whites from the Veneto in north-eastern Italy made from the gargagna grapes with a little trebbiano. This is a merchant's label from a large co-operative that is looking better than it did last year. It has some leesy characters, a creamy texture that enhances its mouthfeel, good weight and a lively dry finish. Exclusive to Vintage Cellars.

2005 Ruffino 'Lumina' Pinot Grigio $14.95

This marks Ruffino's first venture outside Tuscany into the cool northern region of Friuli (near the town of Udine and not far from Venice). Production has soared to 1 million bottles in four vintages. It's an intense, floral white with powerful ripe flavours that reminds me of one of my favourite Asian fruits, the durian. Fine, complex, dry. Exclusive to Vintage Cellars.

2006 Stoneleigh Sauvignon Blanc $20

I like the bright cool fruit of this Marlborough sauvignon more than most. There's pink grapefruit, guava and gooseberry flavours and some flinty, quartzy, minerally characters that gives a sharpness of focus and complexity. Imported by Pernod Ricard.

▭ PRETTY GOOD

2005 Canti Chardonnay Pinot Grigio $8.95

An Italian quaffer with attractive savoury peak skin flavours that has good weight, a pleasant mouthfeel and dry lingering finish. Exclusive to Dan Murphy's.

2006 Corte Giara Pinot Grigio delle Venezie $17.50

The Allegrini family's Corte Giara source this from the Veneto in north-eastern Italy from the hills facing picturesque Lake Garda. It is fresh, clean with savoury, pear-skin characters, mid-palate intensity and an ultra-dry finish. Imported by Negociants.

2006 Concha Y Toro 'Casillero del Diablo' Sauvignon Blanc $13.95

In this case, the wine comes from the Central Valley in Chile. Like the Chardonnay, it doesn't have distinct varietal character but is viscous and textural and so is a fascinating drink. Exclusive to Vintage Cellars.

2006 Montes 'Classic Series' Sauvignon Blanc $9.95

Montes is a major wine company in Chile with its winery at Apalta in the Colchagua Valley. This is a blend of unoaked sauvignon from the Casablanca Valley and Curico that is deliciously different from local or Kiwi examples of the variety. It is smooth, rich and viscous with a dry minerally palate and refreshing zesty acidity. Exclusive to Dan Murphys.

Imported Rosés

▶ BLOODY GOOD

2006 Concha Y Toro 'Casillero del Diablo' Shiraz Rosé $13.95

Sourced from Chile's Central Valley, this is an excellent rosé that is as vibrant as it is brightly pink. There's a touch of complexity from gravelly, savoury notes and pleasing succulence in the mid-palate before a gentle dry finish. Exclusive to Vintage Cellars.

2005 Montana 'East Coast' Rosé $19.50

This is a delightful savoury style that has tangy, wild strawberry flavours, tightness, intensity and finesse before a dry finish that grips the palate. At its best with dishes such as grilled prawns with a chilli tomato sauce. Imported by Pernod Ricard.

2006 Torres 'De Casta' Rosado $14

This stunningly good rosé is made from grenache and carignan sourced from Catalonia. I loved its vibrant intensity, its bright redcurrant, red cherry flavours and clean dry finish. Imported by Negociants.

GOOD

2005 Arrogant Frog Syrah Rosé $9.95

This is the best of the Arrogant Frog range from the South of France: salmon pink, smooth, gentle and savoury; finishing long and dry. Exclusive to Dan Murphys.

2005 Ruffino Rosa di Ninfa $11.95

I'm not sure that anyone wants to know about the nymphs that lie behind the name – it's on the website if you need to know. The wine itself is Tuscan, light pink in colour, soft, round and pleasantly smooth in the mouth, with a savoury dry finish. Exclusive to Vintage Cellars.

PRETTY GOOD

2005 Pascal Delaunay Val de Loire Rosé d'Anjou $9.95

This is a decent savoury rosé from the Anjou region in the Loire Valley: it's a light delicate pink, very smooth in the mouth with some earthy, gravelly characters before a pleasing dry finish. Exclusive to Dan Murphys.

Imported Reds

▶ BLOODY GOOD

2005 Borie de Maurel 'Esprit d'Automne' $15.95

Those of you who saw my two minutes of fame on Rick Stein's *French Odyssey* will understand my affection for the reds of the Minervois, that fabulous southern region close to the walled city of Carcassonne. The 'Spirit of Autumn' is a typical local blend of syrah (40%), carignan and grenache (30% each) and the 2005 is still available. My notes were similar to last year's except that the tannins have softened and the wine is a bit more approachable and delicious enough to warrant an upgrade to 'Bloody Good'. It is rich and concentrated with ripe berry fruit, silky smooth texture and supple, fine, balanced tannins. Exclusive to Vintage Cellars.

2005 Clos Petit Bellane Cotes du Rhone $16.95

This is a good introduction to the wines of the Southern Rhone as it has good typicity – that is, it tastes exactly like the wines of the region should. It is medium-bodied and easy drinking with savoury, earthy, gamey, beetrooty flavours, pleasing vibrance and succulence before a fine, dry finish. Exclusive to Vintage Cellars.

2006 Concha Y Toro 'Casillero del Diablo' Pinot Noir $13.95

Another pleasing Chilean red at a good price, this time from the Casablanca Valley. It's silky smooth, has bright strawberry and red cherry flavours and reasonable variety character. Exclusive to Vintage Cellars.

IMPORTED WINES UNDER $20

2005 Drylands Pinot Noir $23.50

Drylands is a sizeable Marlborough producer that is part of the Nobilo group and is therefore owned by Constellation. This is a clean, fresh, well-made pinot that shows juicy, bright fruit flavours, smooth texture, and a savoury edge. Imported by Hardys.

2005 Henry Fessy 'Domaine des 40 Ecus' Beaujolais Villages $14.90

This is a delicious example of Beaujolais Villages – light- to medium-bodied, supple, silky smooth with good richness and concentration of pure raspberry and strawberry flavours. Imported by Negociants.

★**2005 Portone Valpolicella** $9.95

THE QUAFF 2008 'Another Foreign Affair'
EXOTIC RED WINE OF THE YEAR AWARD

I liked last year's wine and think this is a tad better. It's an unoaked red made from the corvina, rondinella and oseleta of local growers in the Valpolicella region of north-eastern Italy. I enjoy its aromatics, vibrant redcurrant, blackberries and raspberry jube flavours and soft, ripe tannins. An exotic easy-drinking red of this quality for less than $10 – it's a quintessential quaffer. Quaff on! Exclusive to Vintage Cellars.

2006 Stoneleigh Pinot Noir $14.95

This fragrant light-bodied red has good varietal character, delicious ripe dark cherry flavours, silky texture and reasonable length. It's a bit lacking in intensity but still delicious. It will be difficult to find a better pinot at this price point. Imported by Pernod Ricard.

 **GOOD**

2003 Altano $15.70

We're at last starting to see in Australia some of the revival in quality of red table wines from Portugal. This is sourced from the Symington family's vineyards in the breathtakingly beautiful Douro Valley in northern Portugal – close to the town of Oporto. It's made from local varieties tinta roriz and touriga franca. It may need a vigorous swirl to clean up the nose – that's not something to be concerned about. It is rich, concentrated with dark berry flavours, smooth texture and wonderful juiciness on an attractive finish. Imported by Negociants.

2006 Braided River Pinot Noir $18.95

This Marlborough brand is part of the Cheviot Bridge empire and in 2006 offers a smoothly textured pinot with good ripeness, redcurrant and dark cherry flavours made more complex by some savoury notes. Imported by Cheviot Bridge.

2005 Concha Y Toro 'Casillero del Diablo' Cabernet $13.95

Here's something quite different from Chile's Central Valley – rich, deeply flavoured, smoothly texture with complex earthy, leathery notes and plenty of sumptuous tannins. Exclusive to Vintage Cellars.

2005 Concha Y Toro 'Casillero del Diablo' Shiraz $13.95

There's a lot to like about this shiraz from Chile's Central Valley, although it may need some vigorous swirling immediately after it has been opened – or even decanting. It's smooth, almost velvety, with concentrated blackberry and plum flavours and is approachable now even though it has massive tannins to finish. Exclusive to Vintage Cellars.

2006 Mount Riley Pinot Noir $16.95

A pleasing fruit bomb from Marlborough – lashings of ripe strawberries and redcurrants. Imported by Angove's.

2006 Nobilo Merlot $16

This is a smooth, easy-drinking Hawke's Bay merlot that has reasonable richness and concentration of flavour. Imported by Hardys.

PRETTY GOOD

2005 Concha Y Toro 'Casillero del Diablo' Merlot $13.95

This comes from Chile's Central Valley and is soft, round and smooth with fresh garden herbs and some sweet fruit. Exclusive to Vintage Cellars.

2005 Illuminati 'Campirosa' Montepulciano d'Abruzzo $9.95

The Illuminati family has long had large vineyard holdings in Abruzzo devoted to producing montepulciano d'Abruzzo. This may need a swirl or two to tidy it up yet its palate is silky smooth with good weight and complexity and a savoury dry finish. Exclusive to Vintage Cellars.

Lash out

Great-value wines over $15

GREAT-VALUE WINES OVER $15

Most people most of the time, either through necessity or choice, don't want to spend more than $15 on a bottle of wine. And that is clearly the focus of this book. However, there will be times when you can't resist the temptation to spend a bit more – it may be something you do for dinner on weekends or for special occasions, or you might share more expensive bottles with wine-loving friends to expand your knowledge of wines.

So this section of the book contains reviews of more than 100 wines that have a recommended retail price above the $15 limit. You'll find some of these on special below $15 but those that are more expensive will still represent very good value for money. In many cases, I saw them as part of the *Quaff* tastings – and found subsequently that they had a recommended retail price above $15. However, there are many outstanding bargains that I saw as part of my normal work as a wine writer – for *STM* (the *Sunday Times Magazine*) in Perth, the *Bulletin*, *Gourmet Traveller WINE*, the *Qantas Magazine* and *Money Magazine*. I conduct regular new release tastings: when I'm home I taste 30 wines a night on Mondays, Tuesdays and Fridays.

As always with *Quaff*, I am recommending the crème de la crème, the wines that stood out – firstly for reasons of quality, and only secondly because they represent good value.

Buying Wines over $15 – Some Tips

On specials

With changes on the Australian retail scene, especially connected with the expansion of Coles and Woolworths (under all their different shop fronts), nothing stays the same. Discounting and special deals are very much part of daily life. Keep an eye on newspaper advertising to see if any of the wines recommended here are available as specials. You may well find that some of the wines I believe are good value for $18–$20 are available on special below $15, and some that we recommended at $22–$25 are on sale for less than $20. There are no rules, especially with loss leaders. Most liquor stores have 20% (or more) sales on a couple of occasions during the year. Get to know when these are held.

Adopt a wine merchant

There are significant advantages in establishing a relationship with a wine merchant, especially a local one, and channelling all or most of your wine purchases through them. They'll certainly keep you informed of any special deals (whether on price or the availability of rare or difficult-to-get wines). If there are bargains, you'll hear about them first. If those bargains are in short supply, you can expect to be looked after. Another advantage is that the wine merchant will get to know your taste and that will help recommending wines to you. Cultivate the friendship. Once you have found a good wine merchant, never let him or her go.

Sparkling Wines over $15

Chandon Brut $23.95

This is a very attractive bubbly from the Yarra Valley-based Domaine Chandon – the view from its cellar door is one of the most picturesque in the country. The current Brut is lively, pristine and fresh with good intensity, yeasty, lemon citrus characters, creamy in the mid-palate and balanced by zesty acidity.

Bay of Fires 'Tigress' Pinot Noir Chardonnay $22

There's a tremendous range of top-flight wines coming from the northern Tasmanian Bay of Fires winery. This has a softness that makes it very attractive drinking: it has yeasty, lemon sherbert characters before zesty, zingy acidity gives its finish great length.

Starvedog Lane Chardonnay Pinot Noir Pinot Meunier $26

Here is an Adelaide Hills non-vintage bubbly that is very impressive: restrained aromatics, tight structure around a powerful yeasty core, very fine, crisp and dry thanks to taut, vibrant cleansing acidity.

2003 Yarra Burn Pinot Noir Chardonnay $21.95

A Yarra Valley bubbly from Australia's leading sparkling wine producer, Hardys. This has bready, yeasty characters, fascinating complexity, impressive finesse and soft, gentle acidity that lingers.

2003 Yarra Burn Pinot Noir Chardonnay Rosé $21.95

This pinot-dominant blend is one of the wines of the moment, with a growth rate in Australia of about 60% per year. Primarily sourced from the Yarra though topped up with some Tasmanian fruit. It's salmon pink, light, fine and delicate, shows vibrant yeasty characters and a hint of strawberries before a slightly grippy finish that gives a sensation of dryness.

White Wines over $15

2007 Ad Hoc 'Straw Man' Sauvignon Blanc Semillon $18

Former Houghton Chief Winemaker, Larry Cherubino, has established the budget-priced 'Ad Hoc' label, the medium-priced 'The Yard' and flagship 'Cherubino' range – based mostly around the family vineyard at Frankland River. This is a classy Margaret River quaffer – intense passionfruit and white stone-fruit flavours, bright and vibrant, refreshingly cool, with a tiny kick from a hint of new French oak.

2005 Bay of Fires Gewürztraminer $27

Bay of Fires, near Launceston, is the headquarters of Hardys' Tasmanian operation. Talented winemaker Fran Austin is making a great range of table wines under both the 'Bay of Fires' and 'Tigress' labels. This is one of a number of Tassie gewürztraminers setting new standards for Australia. Hedonistically aromatic, even alluring, with honeysuckle, rose petal, Turkish delight characters on the bouquet and the palate. Importantly, there is taut, racy natural acidity, leaving the finish crisp and dry.

2005 Belgravia Chardonnay $18

The Union Bank building in Orange with its superb cafe food, excellent coffee and relaxed ambience is Belgravia's cellar door. Made by David Lowe and Jane Wilson, this is the best chardonnay I've seen from Belgravia and one of the finest from the ultra-cool Orange region. It's complex with neatly integrated cedary oak, cool stone fruit and slatey, minerally characters, impressive finesse, tight structure and refreshing racy acidity.

2006 Brown Brothers Vermentino $16.90

I fell in love with vermentino from Sardinia a couple of years ago in the restaurants of Italy. There, while there's still some warmth in the air, it's a brilliant restaurant white. With the 2006 vintage, Brown Brothers appear to have captured the essence of the variety: it is zesty, refreshingly bright yet savoury, and finishes with taut, quartzy acidity that leaves a trace of bitter almonds.

2006 Clairault Sauvignon Blanc $22

There are some sublime sauvignons coming from the cool, deep south of Margaret River, in the vicinity of Karridale. Yet the region can still make some crackers from its northern reaches. This family winery, with a Caves Road frontage not far from Yallingup, has been revitalised by the winemaking of Will Shields. Here is an excellent example of what it can do in a cool vintage: fragrant, intense, fresh garden herb and green bean flavours, impeccably focused with impressive primary fruit and a clean, lingering passionfruit finish.

2006 Coldstream Hills Chardonnay $26.95

This is the kind of chardonnay that James Halliday would have dreamed of making when he and his wife, Suzannne, started Coldstream Hills in 1985: a wine that shows how well suited the Yarra is to the variety. It has a freshness and vitality, intensity of pure white stone fruit, a juicy succulence, good depth and length. The oak is restrained and the texture creamy and unctuous.

2007 Coriole Fiano $24

On the same trip to Italy where I embraced vermentino, I discovered a great deal about the country's indigenous varieties – and enjoyed them enormously. Perhaps the white wine that impressed me most was fiano, which originally comes from Avelino, in the hills of Campagna in the hinterland of Naples. I got to see a fair bit of

Campagna and its wines and felt that fiano would make a marvellous warm area variety in Australia. This wine (and the first vintage 2005 Coriole) are the best whites I've ever seen from McLaren Vale – even though the vines are still young. The 2007 Coriole Fiano is fragrant and floral, intensely fruity with fresh garden herbs and citrus blossom. It has reasonable weight, is focused and vibrant with crisp, zesty acidity that lingers. First class.

2006 Cumulus 'Climbing' Pinot Gris $19.95

I spent four days in Orange during the year and so I've a fair bit to say about the region. Cumulus, the largest wine company in Orange and a trail-blazer for the region, has two ranges: 'Rolling' at about $16 and 'Climbing' just under $20. The 2006 'Climbing' Pinot Gris has a delicate onion skin/partridge eye colour, is delicate, soft and savoury, tight, fine and very dry with a mouth-puckering finish. Best with food: perhaps a dish of grilled whiting with chips or a delicious nasi goreng.

2006 Cumulus 'Rolling' Chardonnay $16

This shows the hallmarks of its cool-climate origins. Sourced from the part of the Cumulus vineyard that is below 600 metres; above is classified as Orange, below is Central Ranges. Great texture and mouthfeel is the feature of this chardonnay – it's tight, lean and fine, even a touch grippy, certainly cool and refreshing. Restrained, white peach and nectarine flavours. A modern style at a budget price.

2006 D'Arenberg 'The Last Ditch' Viognier $19.95

I generally prefer the D'Arenberg reds to the whites but this strikes a chord: intense, juicy and viscous with some complex, spicy, apricot and cedary oak characters nicely balanced and very drinkable.

2005 Edwards Chardonnay $24

Another very good white from the Edwards family in Margaret River. This is a powerful, complex chardonnay showing cedary oak, lees-stirring, butterscotch and caramel characters and plenty of peachy fruit.

2006 Edwards Semillon Sauvignon Blanc $19

One of the new wave of family wineries in Margaret River (established 1994) with experienced brothers Michael (winemaker) and Christo (viticulturist) looking after the sizeable property south of Wilyabrup while Matilda, their late father Brian's Tiger Moth, keeps guard from her retirement hangar. The Semillon Sauvignon Blanc and Sauvignon Blanc are the best but all wines show gradual improvement. This has vibrance, freshness, intensity of pristine flavours – garden herb and tropical notes – and lively cleansing acidity.

2006 Evans & Tate Chardonnay $20.95

This is the best of the medium-priced Margaret River chardonnays currently available: pristine, fresh with ripe sweet nectarine fruit, restrained cedary oak and crisp, dry, cleansing acidity.

2006 Ferngrove Chardonnay $17.95

A ripe, vibrant, juicy chardonnay from Kim Horton and the team at this Frankland River winery. It has bright, peach, nectarine and melon flavours and a crisp, lively finish.

2006 Fire Gully Chardonnay $24.90

A well-priced yet classy Margaret River chardonnay from Mike Peterkin: delicate, fine, tight and restrained, attractive juicy mouthfeel before fresh dry lingering finish.

2006 Frankland Estate 'Isolation Ridge' Riesling $23
2006 Frankland Estate 'Cooladerra' Riesling $23
2006 Frankland Estate 'Poison Hill' Riesling $23

> Barrie Smith and Judi Cullam and their family at Frankland Estate have been making riesling from their 'Isolation Ridge' vineyard for almost 20 years. In the past few years, they have released individual vineyard wines from two nearby vineyards, Poison Hill and Cooladerra. The current releases are the best yet and are available in a three pack from the winery, although the 'Isolation Ridge' is more widely available. The superb 2006 Frankland Estate 'Isolation Ridge' is tight, restrained and austere yet juicy and powerful with zesty lemon juice. The 2006 'Poison Hill' is succulent with pear and apple flavours and tingly dry acidity while the 'Cooladerra' is plumper and more generous yet still restrained with taut, almost gripping acidity.

2001 Heggies 'Reserve' Riesling $26.95

> Yalumba's Heggies Vineyard high in the Eden Valley consistently makes fine riesling which it sells in the first flush of youth. The same wine is released as a five year old and called 'Reserve'. The 2001 Heggies 'Reserve' has an attractive toasty character, is finely balanced on the cusp between youth and development. It has a core of vibrantly youthful pure lime juice, some minerally complexity and a zesty, dry finish.

2006 Henschke 'Eleanor's Cottage' Sauvignon Blanc Semillon $23

> Anyone with a red wine portfolio as strong as the Henschkes is in danger of having its whites overlooked. I'm marvellously impressed (especially) with the Eden Valley whites – the 'Crane's' Chardonnay, 'Peggy's Hill' Riesling and this delicate, restrained sauvignon blanc semillon. It is pristine and fresh with mouthwatering flavours that persist, before a fine, gentle finish.

GREAT-VALUE WINES OVER $15

2005 Hungerford Hill Tumbarumba Chardonnay $30

The grapes from Tumbarumba, in the foothills of the Snowy Mountains, are much sought after. Hunter winery, Hungerford Hill, has been a keen supporter and won Best Wine at the 2007 New South Wales Wine Awards with this gem: the first time the trophy had not been won by a semillon or a shiraz. This is a complex chardonnay that shows spicy oak, yeasty, leesy, cool melony flavours, creamy texture and fine racy acidity.

2007 Irvine Albarino $25

My favourite Spanish white variety hails from Galicia (especially the region of Rias Baixas) in north-western Spain. Jim Irvine and his winemaking daughter Joanne have captured the essence of the grape in the Eden Valley: this is lifted with apple blossom and pear characters which flow through to the palate. There's succulence, vibrance and fresh, cleansing acidity. Delicious.

2006 Knappstein Semillon Sauvignon Blanc $19

The Clare Valley is an unlikely source of this blend but Knappstein, with winemaker Paul Smith in full flight, is making some excellent wines at present so anything is possible: fresh, lively and floral yet with restrained grapefruit flavours and fine lemony acidity. You may also find the 2007 on the shelves.

2006 Mad Fish Riesling $18

Howard Park makes the early drinking Mad Fish and the leaner, tighter, more austere Howard Park that needs time. This 2006 Mad Fish picked up a gold medal at the Qantas Mount Barker Show. It is intensely lemony with just a hint of lime, is vibrant and juicy with layer after layer of flavour and impressive finesse before a crisp, dry finish that lingers. It's a bargain.

2005 Murray Darling Collection 'Murray Cod' Vermentino $22

Bruce Chalmers has one of Australia's largest vine nurseries near Mildura and has planted small amounts of experimental (especially Italian) varieties to show their potential. This is my favourite of the range – an excellent example of the dry white that excels in the warmth of Sardinia. Savoury, minerally, with a hint of lemon zest and refreshing cleansing acidity. Ideal with roast chicken and a fresh, green salad.

2006 Millbrook Viognier $22

The guys at Millbrook in the Perth Hills have specialised in this increasingly popular white variety. The 2006 is an ethereal white which won two trophies at the Perth Hills Show. Most notably it outscored its sibling, the excellent 2005 Millbrook Shiraz Viognier ($32), making it the first white in an 11 year history to win Wine of the Show. It is wonderfully aromatic with a hint of dried herbs and dried apricot, excellent viscosity, and pristine flavours that linger.

2006 Mitchelton 'Blackwood Park' Riesling $15.95

During his long tenure at Mitchelton former Chief Winemaker, Don Lewis, established a formidable reputation for the consistency and quality of his 'Blackwood Park' Riesling, sourced since 1978 from the estate vineyard at Nagambie Lakes. That, plus its modest retail price, enabled the winery to sell 14 000 cases a year – even when riesling was less fashionable than it is now. The 2005 is delicately floral with rich, powerful grapefruit and lemon citrus flavours before a crisp, dry finish of considerable length. Value, too.

2006 Mountadam Riesling $25

Former Petaluma winemaker, Con Moshos, has found a new lease of life driving this Eden Valley winery in the post–Veuve Clicquot era. Now owned by Adelaide businessman David Brown, Mountadam is looking to refocus and lift wine quality. This first release is a thrilling example of what the Eden Valley does best – a restrained riesling with pristine lemon citrus flavours and slatey, minerally complexity, tight structure and taut, mouth-puckering acidity.

2002 Mount Pleasant 'Elizabeth' Semillon $16.95

This is the very fine current release of one of the Hunter's classic semillons. It continues an unbroken 21-year tradition in which each vintage has won a gold medal or better. There's a hint of toastiness with rich, concentrated lemon, lime citrus flavours that are bold and powerful. Drinking it with oysters gave the texture a marvellous creaminess. Try also the stunning, seamless 1998 Museum Release ($30).

2007 O'Leary Walker 'Polish Hill River' Riesling $17.50

Another outstanding vintage for this brilliantly priced Clare riesling from David O'Leary and Nick Walker: intensely limey, fine even elegant, juicy even succulent, minerally – a classy varietal with depth and length that shows how well the region can do the variety at modest prices.

2006 Plantagenet Riesling $19

As usual, this outstanding Great Southern producer impressed me with its riesling: gentle lemony flavours, hint of lime juice, fresh, delicate and clearly focused.

2006 Sandalford 'Protege' Chardonnay $16.95

This new Margaret River range for Sandalford is positioned between the 'Element' range and their premiums. I'm very impressed with the Classic White, Cabernet Merlot and this unwooded Chardonnay, especially at the price. They certainly enhance Paul Boulden's reputation as one of the West's best winemakers. Delicately floral with lavender aromas, fresh, bright herbal flavours before a soft, fine finish that lingers.

2007 Shaw & Smith Sauvignon Blanc $25

Deserved the market leader after all these years, this is Adelaide Hills sauvignon at its very best. Martin Shaw & Michael Hill Smith seem unable to miss a beat with a terrific taut varietal that has voluminous aromatics, gooseberries and lychees that are just ripe – so still cool and vibrant. This is all the good things about sauvignon blanc – tangy and intense, focused, crisp and dry to finish with some mouth-puckering acidity to entice you to drink (or gulp or sip) the next glass.

2006 Squitchy Lane Chardonnay $30

The name comes from Mike Fitzpatrick's days at Oxford as the AFL Chairman and former Carlton champion launches his Yarra Valley label with a very impressive chardonnay. It is fresh and lively with the bold, pristine flavours of white peach and grapefruit, good viscosity, tight structure and a pleasing aftertaste which lingers. Its small volume is only available by mail order but you can order even a single bottle.

2007 Stella Bella Semillon Sauvignon Blanc $22

A great vintage for Margaret River taken full advantage of by Janice McDonald and the team at Stella Bella. This is bright and lively with good intensity of grassy, herby flavours fleshed out by some cool tropical notes, that finishes fresh and zesty.

2006 Tahbilk Viognier $18.95

Alister Purbrick, the team at this Nagambie Lakes winery, and the sub-region appear to have an affinity with Rhone varietals. This has attractive, lifted apricot flavours that are persistent and deep; there's succulence and weighty viscosity on a multi-layered white.

2005 Taylors 'Jaraman' Riesling $24.95

For me, this has been the best wine yet under the mid-priced label of the Clare Valley's largest producer, Taylors. Atypically, as most of Taylors wines are proudly Clare, this is a blend of Eden Valley and Clare riesling that is aromatic, intensely limey, clean, fresh and fine. It is packed with layer after layer of mouth-puckering flavour before a vibrant finish that lingers.

2006 Keith Tulloch Chardonnay $26

This new release from fourth-generation Hunter vigneron Keith Tulloch's tiny family winery serves as a timely reminder of just how good the region's chardonnay can be. It's made from low-yielding old vines and given de luxe treatment – 100% barrel-fermentation in new oak without showing overt oak character. There is a pure core of cool fruity chardonnay (white peach, nectarine) and spicy, minerally complexity, held together by tight structure and taut, racy acidity.

2006 Wairau River Sauvignon Blanc $25.95

Not cheap but quality Kiwi sauvignon with intense ripe passionfruit, lychees and gooseberry flavours, bracing zesty acidity. Classy.

2006 Windance Semillon Sauvignon Blanc $18

A small producer from Yallingup which impresses: this has lively aromatics, green pea and green bean flavours, vibrant freshness and cleansing natural acidity.

2005 Xabregas 'Show Reserve' Chardonnay $20

While I'm not generally a fan of Mount Barker chardonnay, Di Miller has made a wine to shake my conviction. This has restrained oak, cool green-skinned flavours, is tight and focused with a lively finish.

Pink Wines over $15

2007 Bay of Fires 'Tigress' Rosé $25.50

> A bright youthful rosé from Tassie made by Fran Austin which shows strawberry and red cherry characters, admirable zestiness before taut, bracing acidity that enables it to finish crisp and dry.

2007 Brookland Valley 'Verse 1' Rosé $15.90

> A brilliant rosé that deservedly picked up a gold medal at the Melbourne Show, this is vibrant with raspberry flavours and a long dry tanginess to finish.

2006 Logan 'Hannah' Rosé $20

> Logan source this from a family vineyard in Orange, crush the shiraz grapes and run it off after 12 hours, giving it a restrained yet bright pink colour. There's sweet strawberry, redcurrant and red cherry flavours, softness in the mid-palate which makes it very easy drinking before a gently dry finish.

2007 Charles Melton Rose of Virginia $20

> This Barossa gem will, once again, be one of the country's best rosés – made predominantly from grenache with some shiraz, cabernet sauvignon and a touch of pinot meunier. While naturally dedicated to Charlie's wife, the name echoes that of the nearby hamlet of Virginia. It's delicately fragrant, has heaps of pure sweet redcurrant and strawberry fruit, is focused, tight and vibrant, before a clean, crisp, dry finish.

2006 Plantagenet 'Eros' Rosé $16.50

> Made mainly from merlot sourced from the Great Southern and Pemberton, this is a fresh, clean vibrant rosé, with delicate ripe redcurrant flavours and pleasing sweetness balanced by lively acidity.

Red Wines over $15

2004 Bella Ridge Cabernet Shiraz $18

Seek out these new guys in the Swan Valley! This is soft, full-bodied and fleshy with seductive, lush flavours.

2005 Bella Ridge Tempranillo $21

A new Swan Valley producer who impresses with this robust Spanish varietal: try with a stir-fry of beef and black bean sauce.

2005 Bimbadgen Shiraz $24.95

The Hunter Valley's Bimbadgen is probably best known for its restaurant and cellar door which are among the region's best. Their latest-release shiraz came up well in an extensive tasting of Hunter shiraz from the 2005 vintage. It is medium-bodied, has savoury brambly characters, impressive richness and depth in the mid-palate, and substantial, ripe, fine-grained tannins. Match it with a perfect sirloin and a powerful shiraz-based sauce.

2005 Bowen Estate Cabernet Sauvignon $28

With Coonawarra being so important to Australia's biggest companies, there is a tendency for these guys to dominant the landscape. Thanks heavens for the family wineries – people like the Bowens, the Balnaves, the Lynns, the Hollicks and the Zemas – which are the lifeblood (and for wine writers the hospitable heart) of the region. Daughter Emma has taken some of the hard work off the shoulders of Doug and Joy – not that their pace has slackened any – while son Simon is chef/owner (with his partner Erika Burg) at Pipers of Penola, one of the region's finest. This is a fantastic vintage for the region so no one is surprised at how good this is: gently fragrant, opulent, concentrated spice and blackcurrant flavours with a hint of mint. There's neatly integrated cedary oak, too, to provide structure for ageing. That will also be helped by the substantial ripe tannins. For all that, it has languid sweet fruit, finesse and succulence to makes it approachable in the short term – especially with veal rib eye and a robust cabernet jus.

2005 Coriole Sangiovese $19.95

The McLaren Vale seems admirably suited to sangiovese and having mature vines shows through. Compared to a chianti, it appears more fruit sweet yet it has a savoury edge. The generous texture is a high point – it's soft, smooth and fleshy. Gentle tannin grip to finish. In short supply. The 2006 has also been released.

2005 Cumulus 'Climbing' Cabernet Sauvignon $19.95

I've not been a great fan of cabernet from Orange, so I'm doubly impressed by this cool-climate varietal sourced from the 508 ha Cumulus vineyard by Philip Shaw and his team. There's intense blackcurrant and mulberry flavours, supple tongue-coatingly smooth thickly viscous texture and restrained fine tannins. Cellar for the short term or drink now with a robust, slow-cooked dish of lamb shanks in red wine sauce.

2005 D'Arenberg 'D'Arry's Original' Shiraz Grenache $20

Named for D'Arenberg's patriach, the spritely d'Arry Osborn, this traditional red blend is sourced from old vines on the family's vineyards and shows the depth of flavour you'd expect. The 2005 is quite tightly structured, even firm, with impressive weight, and rich, concentrated briary, dark berry, allspice and dark chocolate flavours. While approachable now, I expect it to soften with short-term cellaring.

2005 Georges Duboeuf Chiroubles $23

In another age, Beaujolais was everyone's favourite before a drop off in quality led the region towards virtual oblivion. Top producers such as Duboeuf have been working hard to claw back the market: so it's great to see a delightful, quality Beaujolais cru such as this. Wonderfully aromatic, intensely fruity (think blackcurrant pastille) and succulent yet with a pleasing grip to finish. At its best with food – say roasted free-range chicken.

2004 Evans & Tate Margaret River Cabernet Merlot $19.95

A rare red from the region which is made in sufficient volume to keep its price down. It is unctuous, almost velvety with an excellent mouthfeel. Its oakiness is matched by dark plum and blackcurrant flavours and ripe, approachable tannins.

2006 Faber Petit Verdot $19.50

One of Australia's best warm-climate petit verdot comes from this family winery in the Swan Valley: ripe sweet fruit, fresh raspberry and bitter chocolate, fine tight tannins.

2005 Ferngrove 'Majestic' Cabernet Sauvignon $24.95

Frankland River in WA's deep south has produced a cabernet worthy of standing alongside Houghton's 'Jack Mann' with this bewilderingly good show-stopper: Best Wine at the 2006 Qantas Mount Barker Show. It's a fresh elegant red with bright sweet blackcurrant flavours, lush and velvety texture, and gentle fine tannins.

2005 Forester Cabernet Merlot $19

Even at this price, Kevin McKay can draw some elegance from his Margaret River fruit: succulent, rich and concentrated, with some restrained firmness to finish.

2003 Freeman Rondinella Corvina $35

The two red varieties – rondinella and corvina – hail from Northern Italy's Veneto which vigneron Brian Freeman likens in climate, topography and cherry production to the Hilltops region around Young. This is a big complex and savoury blend with tarry, earthy, charcuterie characters, wonderful generosity and succulence, and substantial yet restrained tannins that grip gently. Perfect with osso buco.

2005 Heartland Cabernet Sauvignon $17

What you're looking for at this price is drinkability: here is a blend from Langhorne Creek and the Limestone Coast – and winemaker Ben Glaetzer – which delivers just that. It's juicy, succulent, almost syrupy smooth with redcurrant jube and blackcurrant flavours before a gentle finish that lingers.

2005 Kaesler 'Stonehorse' Shiraz $28

While the Kaesler vineyards in the Barossa date back more than 100 years, this wine company led by winemaker Reid Bosward was only established at the end of the 20th century. Shiraz is a highlight: 'Old Vine' ($60) and 'The Bogan' ($50) impress. So, too, does the more modestly priced 'Stonehorse': deep, concentrated flavours, ripe opulent dark berry fruit, vanillin oak, immense power, velvety texture and substantial ripe tannins.

2005 Kingston 'Empiric' Petit Verdot $18.95

Petit verdot is a robust winter red that deserves to be more popular. It has an affinity to the warm regions along the Murray where it has been championed by Bill Moularadellis who has 100 ha in one Kingston vineyard. This has great softness, generosity and richness of dark berry flavour, attractive velvety texture, substantial fine-grained tannins and a lush, gentle finish lifted by acidity.

2004 Lamont's Shiraz $24

One of the Swan Valley's top producers is producing consistently good shiraz. This is quite robust and oaky with good depth, power and rich, ripe plummy flavours. I'm expecting it to settle with another few months bottle age as the oak becomes more integrated.

2004 Peter Lehmann Cabernet Merlot $18

While the Barossa is not a great region for cabernet, it can produce some excellent quaffing wines in a good vintage like this. The team from Peter Lehmann have fashioned a deeply viscous, slippery red with dark cherry and blackcurrant flavours and fine ripe tannins.

2004 Majella Cabernet Sauvignon $30

Majella has had one of Coonawarra's most consistent and best-performed cabernets over the past decade. Eight trophies underline what a brilliant vintage 2004 was: opulent and powerful, deep and lavishly flavoured, lush and velvety. Needs time but is supple enough to reward even the impatient.

2006 Majella 'The Musician' Cabernet Shiraz $18

One of Coonawarra's best wineries has had enormous success with this early drinking red. I love its gluggability. There's refreshing balance between having enough character and depth of flavour to be interesting and being approachable when young. Amazingly considering its price, the 2005 has just won two trophies at the London International Wine Challenge. The 2006 is delicately perfumed, silky smooth and succulent.

2003 Geoff Merrill 'Jacko's Blend' Shiraz $23.50

Geoff Merrill knows how to handle McLaren Vale shiraz – witness his 'Henley' Shiraz and Jimmy Watson Trophy win with his 2004 'Reserve' Shiraz. Here's what he can do with a four-year-old shiraz at a more user-friendly price point. This has attractive brambly oak, concentrated redcurrant and dark plum flavours with some tarry notes, thick viscous texture and moderate balanced tannins.

2005 Mitchelton Shiraz $21

The warmth of Central Victoria spawns this aromatic, lively shiraz with spicy, dark plum and black cherry flavours and smooth approachability.

2005 Mount Trio 'Gravel Pit' Shiraz Viognier $19.95

A highly successful Porongurups label. With wines like this, it's easy to see why: deeply flavoured with ripe plummy fruit and heaps of oak, fleshy, viscous and very drinkable.

2005 Nepenthe 'Tryst' Cabernet Sauvignon Tempranillo Zinfandel $15.95

This fine Adelaide Hills producer, now owned by McGuigan Simeon, is best known for its alluring sauvignon blanc. While I'm not a fan of cabernet from the region, winemaker Michael Fogarty has put together a quirky blend (70:25:5) that works extremely well in this vintage. Attractive spicy, sweet redcurrant and wild cherry flavours with some savoury notes and a pleasing dry finish that lingers.

2005 Oatley 'Wild Oats' Shiraz Viognier $18.95

This is stage one in the resurrection of Bob Oatley and his family, post Rosemount, post Southcorp: the name of their Sydney–Hobart yacht given a new lease of life from a winery operation centred around Mudgee. Here is a decent, good-value red – a touch too pruney for me, but silky smooth, rich with ripe sweet fruit and a gentle, slightly porty, finish.

GREAT-VALUE WINES OVER $15

2004 Parker 'Terra Rossa' Cabernet Sauvignon $34.95

If money is no object, drink this while waiting five to ten years for the Parker 'First Growth' ($80) to come around. Otherwise, just enjoy this seductive, generous, velvety textured, lush and richly concentrated cabernet when you need something memorable for a winter's evening.

2005 Penley Estate 'Condor' Shiraz Cabernet $18.95

I've tasted some excellent Coonawarra reds from Kym Tolley recently, including a quartet from 2005 at the same price point: the seductively ripe 'Hyland' Shiraz, a good (though tannic) 'Phoenix' Cabernet, and this 'Condor' blend of shiraz (60%) and cabernet sauvignon (40%). While the 'Condor' is big and alcoholic (15%), it has a depth of rich concentrated fruit, silky smooth texture and fine, ripe tannins. Balanced, easy drinking.

2005 Penley Estate 'Gryphon' Merlot $18.95

Coonawarra merlot is Australia's best – and it need not be expensive. Enjoy with roasted veal shoulder with roast vegetables and a red wine jus.

2005 Penley Estate 'Phoenix' Cabernet Sauvignon $18.95

A budget-priced Coonawarra cabernet from the excellent performers at Penley Estate: concentrated blackcurrant flavours with supple, approachable tannins.

2004 Pirramimma 'Stocks Hill' Shiraz $18

The budget range from an excellent McLaren Vale producer offers ripe plum and redcurrant flavours and an easy-drinking style.

2005 Primo Estate 'Il Briccone' Shiraz Sangiovese $22

You can't shake the Italian heritage (or the Maserati) out of Joe Grilli which is celebrated in this blend, nicknamed 'Il Briccone' (the rogue). The noble Tuscan grape sangiovese (45%) adds a savoury dryness to the spicy, fleshy, generously flavoured Aussie shiraz from the Grilli vineyards close to Adelaide. Vibrant, gluggable, say with a ragu bolognese, spaghetti, or lamb meatballs.

2004 Punt Road Shiraz $25

Although the Yarra Valley built its reputation on chardonnay, pinot noir and cabernet, there has been some superb shiraz made in recent times, especially by Yering Station and De Bortoli. Under winemaker Kate Goodman, Punt Road has established a reputation for producing very good wines at fair prices – like this cooler-climate shiraz which has dense, ripe plummy fruit, pleasing complexity, smooth texture and balanced ripe tannins.

2005 Rutherglen Estate Durif $17.95

Winemaker Nicole Esdaile is making some terrific wines (especially the reds) at this newish, sizeable Rutherglen winery. She picked up a gold medal for this wine at the Alternative Varieties Show in Mildura. It's a fruit-driven style that is deep and rich with concentrated dark berry flavours, smooth yet chewy texture and characteristic ripe, substantial tannins. Needs a hearty, slow-cooked lamb shanks dish to look at its best.

2004 Seppelt 'Moyston' Cabernet Merlot $29.95

A much-loved style, first made by the legendary Colin Preece in 1951, and named after a small town near Great Western. This relaunch of the grand old label is based on cabernet sauvignon from Great Western and cabernet and merlot from Bendigo. It has great richness, concentration and depth of flavour, is wonderfully smooth and balanced, with neat integration of fruit and oak. Satisfying.

2005 Shaw & Smith Shiraz $38

The Adelaide Hills is turning heads (well, mine at least) with superb cool-climate shiraz from the likes of Shaw & Smith, Petaluma and Wolf Blass 'Platinum Label'. The 2005 Shaw & Smith is a fine, elegantly structured red with seductive velvety texture, deep, powerful, ultra-concentrated brambly, mulberry flavours and ripe, fine-grained tannins. There's harmony, too, and an element of restraint.

2004 Taminick Cellars 'Premium' Shiraz $16

This year, I've tasted the range of wines from Booth's Taminick, which has been at its Glenrowan vineyard and winery for a hundred years. It has vines still in production that were planted in 1919. This is a quaffer's paradise as all the wines available from their cellar door are $16 or less with the exception of the Centenary Port ($55), which celebrates their 100 year history. I should point out that Taminick Cellars have a reputation for producing powerful, full-bodied reds with massive tannins. My favourite of the wines I've seen so far is the more expensive shiraz ($16) made from 84-year-old vines. The 2004 Taminick Cellars 'Premium' Shiraz has spicy, vanillin oak fragrance, ripe blackberry flavours, lashings of oak and substantial tannins. There is some firmness on the finish, but especially with robust meat dishes such as lamb shanks, the wine is quite approachable. At 16°, it is higher in alcohol than most. It could happily be cellared for five to ten years depending on how good the cellaring was.

2005 Tarrawarra 'Tin Cows' Pinot Noir $25

Tarrawarra, consistently one of the Yarra's best pinot producers, decided not to make a red under their label from the 2005 vintage and so winemaker Clare Halloran has declassified it into their second label,

Tin Cows. The benefit to this wine is palpable: persistent dark cherry flavours with rich earthy characters, impeccably balanced and textural before a gentle, savoury finish.

2004 Tatachilla Cabernet Sauvignon $22.95

This is a decent McLaren Vale cabernet at a fair price – deep dark berry flavours, very smooth and juicy.

2004 Were Cabernet Sauvignon $25

Another new producer from Margaret River hits the heights with a quality cabernet: fine, elegant red with concentrated rich blackcurrant and red cherry flavours, fleshy texture, and fine ripe tannins.

2005 West Cape Howe Cabernet Merlot $17.50

Anything but a shrinking violet from the lads at Denmark's West Cape Howe winery: robust, vanilla bean and coconutty oak and powerful dark berry flavours. Ideal for the barbecue.

2004 Willow Bridge Shiraz Viognier $28

A red to delight from the Ferguson Valley's largest producer: smoky oak, fleshy, almost lush texture, wonderfully ripe deep flavours, balanced with fine supple tannins.

2005 Windance Shiraz $18

This shiraz from near Yallingup is almost as good as its more expensive 'Reserve' sibling; robust and oaky yet densely flavoured, smooth and drinkable, preferably with a big steak.

2005 Wolf Blass 'Yellow Label' Shiraz $16.95

Outstanding value from Wolf Blass: fragrant, ripe plummy flavours tame vanillin oak and substantial tannins to produce a soft, smooth and easy-drinking red.

2006 Yalumba 'Bush Vine' Grenache $16.95

You have to love the Barossa Valley and great old family companies like Yalumba for being able to source a wine such as this from low-yielding, 70-year-old bush vines and sell it so cheaply. Frankly, it's delicious: brambly, red berry characters, succulent, silky smooth texture, deep raspberry juice vibrance and pleasing approachability. Think tomato-based pasta sauce and Wiech's egg noodles from the Barossa.

2003 Zema 'Cluny' $25.60

They're celebrating the Zema 30th anniversary in style – with a terrific range of Coonawarra reds. This blend of cabernet sauvignon (60%), merlot (23%), cabernet franc (9%) and malbec (8%) is delicately scented, supple, round and fleshy with rich, concentrated, ripe red berry fruit, seamlessly integrated oak and substantial yet approachable tannins.

Sweet and Fortified Wines over $15

SWEET WINES

2006 Tim Adams Botrytis Riesling $20

A delightful sticky from one of the Clare Valley's top producers: gently fragrant, wonderful sweet and viscous with intense lemon–lime citrus flavours and crisp cleansing acidity.

2006 D'Arenberg Noble Chardonnay Semillon $20

I thought this was fabulous: alluring, ripe apricot and peach flavours, soft, seductive creamy texture, sweet and unctuous yet finishing fresh and crisp thanks to its pristine cleansing acidity.

FORTIFIED WINES

All Saints Rutherglen Muscat $19.50

This is much improved from the previous occasion on which I saw the wine and has obviously been freshened up. There's a freshness and vibrance about it that combines depth of flavour and lush sweetness with a lightness of touch that entices you to have one as a nightcap. Malt and toffee flavours, sweet lush texture, crisp drying finish.

All Saints Rutherglen Tokay $19.50

An excellent entry-level fortified – gently syrupy, sweet malt, honey and toffee, some depth yet bright, fresh and light.

Campbell's Classic Muscat $39.10

A serious Rutherglen muscat at a fair price: fragrant, deeply raisiny flavours, velvety almost lush texture, vibrant and bright to finish.

Campbell's Rutherglen Tokay $18.35

As sometimes happens with good fortifieds, this needed a bit of a swirl when it was opened. Then it is fresh and lively with deep sweetness, honey and golden syrup flavour and a seductive finish.

Hugh Hamilton 'The Ruffian' Liqueur Muscat $24.50

This was a bit of a surprise packet, a classy McLaren Vale fortified to give the Rutherglen guys some competition. It has intense malt, butterscotch and raisin flavours, is soft, round and vibrant and finishes clean and fresh.

Morris Classic Muscat $18.95

Often referred to as the canister muscat (because it is sold in a canister), this is one of the best-value muscats of them all: intense, raisiny, complex with layer after layer of flavour, silky smooth texture and good weight. With all that, it's pristine, fresh and vibrant and tempts you towards one more glass.

Pfeiffers Classic Tokay $24.50

Fragrant, butterscotch, treacle and golden syrup flavours with weight and depth yet finesse and a lightness of touch.

Pfeiffers Rutherglen Tokay $16.90

This is an excellent entry-level tokay that appears to have a darker colour than many. There's honey, butterscotch and malt, depth and richness of flavour and a lightness of touch that sets the best apart.

Seppelt 'DP 63' Grand Muscat $26.95

This is memorable because of its fantastic lush, velvety texture, butterscotch and toffee flavours and lingering vibrance.

SWEET AND FORTIFIED WINES OVER $15

Stanton & Killeen Classic Muscat $25

Chris Killeen was a leading fortified winemaker from Rutherglen who died this year at the far too early age of 52. He was a port obsessive who made some of the country's best ports in a much more savoury (more Portuguese) style than has been usual. Chris was influential in many ways and a quiet, measured, and thoroughly delightful man. Celebrate his life with this thick, lush, deep and powerful muscat and admire its lively acidity which allows you to relish its sweetness without ever becoming cloying.

Stanton & Killeen Classic Tokay $25

Deep cold tea, malt and toffee flavours, wonderfully syrupy, sweet, fine, elegant and long.

Talijancich 'Julian James' Red Liqueur $29

James Talijancich excels with aged verdelho, makes Australia's best graciano, and a range of first-rate fortifieds which are what the Swan does best. This is both beguiling and seductive: wonderfully lush, viscous and weighty on the palate with pure red berry fruit flavours that linger with fine spirit.

How to track down the bargains

HOW AND WHERE TO BUY GREAT-VALUE WINE

If you're keen on finding bargains in bottleshop land, one of the best things you can do is make a nuisance of yourself – in the nicest possible way, of course. Make sure the people behind the counter at your favourite wine retailer know you're interested in drinking good wine, and are looking out for bargains. If they're doing their job properly, they should nurture you as a valued customer – you buying cheap wine on a regular basis is just as important as one-off sales of stratospherically priced icon wines to people who'll never come back.

As a wine consumer, you have two choices. You can either sit back and let the wine shops seduce you into buying this week's unbeatable special through their advertising and their promotions and their smooth talking. Or you can make a little bit of effort and discover your own specials all by yourself. Here are a few tips to help you become a well-informed, quick-thinking, quick-quaffing wine bargain explorer.

Some Tips for the Bargain Hunter

Read about wine
Yeah, I know the old saying, 'don't believe everything you read', but in the cause of finding good value, I reckon you should take notice of at least some of the many thousands of words published about wine in newspapers, magazines and over the internet each week.

Gaining knowledge about how wines are made, where they come from, why they taste different, and what foods go well with them, will help you become a more discerning consumer.

One way to keep *Quaff 2008* up to date throughout the next year is to become a subscriber to the *Quaff* website at **www.quaff.com.au**. **It's free** to join and we'll send you weekly reviews of the latest great-value wines as soon as they hit the market. Quaff on!

Buy up big
In the short term, buying wines by the case, or dozen bottles, can be a real pain in the back pocket. But I thoroughly recommend it, as you are almost guaranteed to receive a discount. If you can't afford it yourself, get together with a group of mates and each chip in the cost of a couple of bottles – that way you spread the cost but share the benefits. Maybe it's a sign of the times but many retailers will also offer a better price to customers who buy half a dozen bottles at a time.

Where the bloody hell are you?
No amount of reading beats experience. Most Australians live a few hours' drive from a wine region. There's no excuse not to get into the car and visit a couple of cellar doors. Australia's winemakers want to know where you are and, if you're not out and about visiting them, why not?

At the cellar doors, you'll (hopefully) get an idea of how to taste wine for maximum enjoyment, and you'll be able to (hopefully) learn about how grapes are grown. Cellar doors are also great places to find discounted wines – bargain bins, ends of vintage, reduced to clear, often on tasting before you buy. Many wineries have mailing lists that you can join, and offer exclusive bargains to mailing list members. If you can't visit a cellar door, then many wine shops have in-store tastings, and wine exhibitions are enjoying increasing popularity.

Spend more money

You probably don't expect to be told this in a book dedicated to finding the most enjoyment for the least expense, but a big tip is to try and spend a little bit more on wine than you did last time (within reason, of course, and without plunging yourself into debt … although I can talk). If you're used to spending $6, try a $9.95 bottle of the same variety or style next time you visit the bottleshop; if $10 is your usual spend, lash out on a $15 bottle – and so on. Another idea is to buy these slightly more expensive bottles once a week for a special Friday or Saturday dinner or a long Sunday lunch with friends. You may very well think that the extra money isn't worth it – in which case, revert to the old favourites and save yourself some cash. But you may also find that the slightly pricier wines can offer better value for money – in other words, by increasing your spend by 20%, you can increase your enjoyment by 100%. You won't know, though, unless you try for yourself.

Don't believe the hype

Be very careful out there. Australian wine marketing departments are incredibly clever at attaching little shiny round stickers to their labels that look uncannily like medals won at some wine show or other. Don't be fooled. Read the shiny stickers carefully. If they tell you the wine has won two bronze medals, it means it was judged to be fair to average quality on two separate occasions. If they tell you the winery was judged Winery of the Year at some international drinks fair in Finland in 1986, be cautious. And even if they tell you that the wine in the bottle has won a string of gold medals and trophies, while you can be safe that the wine is well made, that's no guarantee you will like it. Again – and again and again – try before you buy, if you can.

Finding the Wines

This index will enable you to source further information on any of the wines reviewed in *Quaff*, such as your nearest local stockist. The name by which the wine is known (the winery or label) is followed by the name of the distributor (where appropriate), a website or email address and a contact number.

AD HOC (LARRY CHERUBINO WINES)
www.larrycherubino.com   (08) 6364 4838

ALASIA (NEGOCIANTS)
www.negociantsaustralia.com   (08) 8112 4210

ALKOOMI
www.alkoomiwines.com.au   (08) 9855 2229

ALL SAINTS
www.allsaintswine.com.au   (02) 6035 2222

ALTANO (NEGOCIANTS)
www.negociantsaustralia.com   (08) 8112 4210

A MANO (TREMBATH & TAYLOR)
virginia@trembathandtaylor.com.au   (03) 9696 7018

ANGOVE'S
www.angoves.com.au   (08) 8580 3100

ANGAS BRUT (YALUMBA)
www.yalumba.com   (08) 8112 4200

ANVERS
www.anvers.com.au   (08) 8323 9603

ARROGANT FROG (DAN MURPHY'S)
www.danmurphys.com.au   1300 723 388

BACK VINTAGE
www.backvintage.com.au   1300 789 640

BAILY & BAILY (WOOLWORTHS LIQUOR)
thunt@woolworths.com.au   (02) 8885 1771

BANROCK STATION (HARDY WINE COMPANY)
www.hardywines.com.au   1800 088 711

BARKING OWL (MILLBROOK)
www.millbrookwinery.com.au   (08) 9525 5796

BAY OF FIRES (HARDY WINE COMPANY)
www.hardywines.com.au									1800 088 711

BELGRAVIA
www.unionbank.com.au									(02) 6361 4441

BELLA RIDGE
www.bellaridge.com.au									(08) 9250 4962

BETHANY
www.bethany.com.au									(08) 8563 2086

BIMBADGEN
www.bimbadgen.com.au									(02) 4998 7585

BLACK CHOOK (PENNY'S HILL)
www.pennyshill.com.au									(08) 8556 4460

BLEASDALE
www.bleasdale.com.au									(08) 8537 3001

BORIE DE MAUREL (VINTAGE CELLARS)
www.vintagecellars.com.au								1300 366 084

BOWEN
www.bowenestate.com.au									(08) 8737 2229

BRAIDED RIVER (CHEVIOT BRIDGE)
www.cheviotbridge.com.au								(03) 8656 7000

BROOKLAND VALLEY (HARDY WINE COMPANY)
www.hardywines.com.au									1800 088 711

BROWN BROTHERS
www.brown-brothers.com.au								(03) 5720 5500

CAMPBELLS
www.campbellswine.com.au								(02) 6032 9458

CANTI (DAN MURPHY'S)
www.danmurphys.com.au									1300 723 388

CAPEL VALE
www.capelvale.com									(08) 9727 0105

CARD COLLECTION (SIMON GILBERT)
www.simongilbertwines.com.au								(02) 6376 1245

CATCHING THIEVES (MCWILLIAM'S)
www.mcwilliams.com.au									1800 800 584

CHALK HILL
www.chalkhill.com.au									(08) 8556 2121

FINDING THE WINES 219

CHAMBERS
www.chambersrosewood.com.au (02) 6032 8641

CHANDON
www.domainechandon.com.au (03) 9739 110

CHARLES MELTON
www.charlesmeltonwines.com.au (08) 8563 3606

CLAIRAULT
www.clairaultwines.com.au (08) 9755 6655

CLOS PETITE BELLANE (VINTAGE CELLARS)
www.vintagecellars.com.au 1300 366 084

COCKATOO RIDGE (FINE WINE PARTNERS)
www.finewinepartners.com 1300 668 512

COLDSTONE (VICTORIAN ALPS WINERY)
www.victorianalpswinery.com (03) 5751 1992

COLDSTREAM HILLS (FOSTER'S)
www.fostersgroup.com 1300 651 650

COMMISSIONERS BLOCK (ROBERTS ESTATE)
www.robertsestatewines.com (03) 5024 5704

CONCHA Y TORO (VINTAGE CELLARS)
www.vintagecellars.com.au 1300 366 084

COOKOOTHAMA (NUGAN ESTATE)
www.nuganestate.com.au (02) 6962 1822

CORIOLE
www.coriole.com (08) 8323 8305

CORTE GIARA (NEGOCIANTS)
www.negociantsaustralia.com (08) 8112 4210

CROSS COUNTRY (BEELGARA)
www.beelgaraestate.com.au 1800 171 154

CUMULUS
www.cumuluswines.com.au (02) 6390 7900

D'ARENBERG
www.darenberg.com.au 1800 882 335

DEAKIN ESTATE
www.deakinestate.com.au (03) 5029 1666

DE BORTOLI
www.debortoli.com.au (02) 9636 6033

DEVIL'S LAIR (FOSTER'S)
www.fostersgroup.com 1300 651 650

DRYLANDS (HARDY WINE COMPANY)
www.hardywines.com.au — 1800 088 711

EARTHWORKS (LANGMEIL)
www.langmeilwinery.com.au — (08) 8563 2595

EDWARDS
www.edwardsvineyard.com.au — (08) 9755 5999

EVANS & TATE (MCWILLIAM'S)
www.mcwilliams.com.au — 1800 800 584

FABER
johngriffiths@iinet.net.au — (08) 9296 0619

FERNGROVE
www.ferngrove.com.au — (08) 9227 0297

FIRE GULLY (PIERRO)
pierro@iinet.net.au — (08) 9755 6220

FIRESTICK (POOLE'S ROCK)
www.poolesrock.com.au — (02) 9563 2500

FISHBONE (BLACKWOOD)
www.fishbonewines.com — (08) 9756 0088

FISHER'S CIRCLE (FOSTER'S)
www.fostersgroup.com — 1300 651 650

FLAGSTONE (VINTAGE CELLARS)
www.vintagecellars.com.au — 1300 366 084

FORESTER
www.foresterestate.com.au — (08) 9755 2788

FOUR SISTERS (TAHBILK)
www.tahbilk.com.au — (03) 5794 2555

FOX CREEK
www.foxcreekwines.com — (08) 8556 2403

FRAMINGHAM (PERNOD RICARD)
www.pernod-ricard-pacific.com — 1300 363 153

FRANKLAND
www.franklandestate.com.au — (08) 9855 1544

FREEMAN
www.freemanvineyards.com.au — (02) 6384 4299

FREIXENET (BACARDI LION)
www.freixenet.com.au — 1800 357 994

GEMTREE
www.gemtreevineyards.com.au — (08) 8323 8199

GEOFF MERRILL
www.geoffmerrillwines.com (08) 8381 6877

GEORGES DUBOEUF (NEGOCIANTS)
www.negociantsaustralia.com (08) 8112 4210

GIESEN (NEGOCIANTS)
www.negociantsaustralia.com (08) 8112 4210

GNANGARA (MCWILLIAM'S)
www.mcwilliams.com.au 1800 800 584

GOLDEN GATE (ICON BRANDS)
www.mirandawines.com.au (02) 8345 6307

GRANT BURGE
www.grantburgewines.com.au (08) 8563 7522

GROWERS
www.thegrowers.com (08) 9755 2121

HANGING ROCK
www.hangingrock.com.au (03) 5427 0542

HARDYS (HARDY WINE COMPANY)
www.hardywines.com.au 1800 088 711

HASELGROVE (VINTAGE CELLARS)
www.vintagecellars.com.au 1300 366 084

HENRY FESSY (NEGOCIANTS)
www.negociantsaustralia.com (08) 8112 4210

HENSCHKE
www.henschke.com.au (08) 8564 8223

HOUGHTON (HARDY WINE COMPANY)
www.hardywines.com.au 1800 088 711

HUGEL (NEGOCIANTS)
www.negociantsaustralia.com (08) 8112 4210

HUGH HAMILTON
www.hughhamiltonwines.com.au (08) 8323 8689

HUNGERFORD HILL
www.hungerfordhill.com.au (02) 4998 7375

ILLUMINATI (VINTAGE CELLARS)
www.vintagecellars.com.au 1300 366 084

INNOCENT BYSTANDER (FINE WINE PARTNERS)
www.finewinepartners.com 1300 668 512

IRVINE
www.irvinewines.com.au (08) 8564 1046

JACOB'S CREEK (PERNOD RICARD)
www.pernod-ricard-pacific.com   1300 363153

JANE BROOK
www.janebrook.com.au   (08) 9274 1432

JEAN PIERRE (DE BORTOLI)
www.debortoli.com.au   (02) 9636 6033

JIM BARRY
jbwines@jimbarry.com   (08) 8842 2261

KAESLER
www.kaesler.com.au   (08) 8562 4488

KAISER STUHL (FOSTER'S)
www.fostersgroup.com   1300 651 650

KEITH TULLOCH
www.keithtullochwine.com.au   (02) 4998 7500

KILLAWARRA (FOSTER'S)
www.fostersgroup.com   1300 651 650

KINGSTON ESTATE
www.kingstonestatewines.com   (08) 8130 4500

KIRRIHILL
www.kirrihillwines.com.au   (08) 8842 1233

KNAPPSTEIN (FINE WINE PARTNERS)
www.finewinepartners.com   1300 668 512

KOONARA
www.koonara.com   1300 558 187

LACHLAN RIDGE (VINTAGE CELLARS)
www.vintagecellars.com.au   1300 366 084

LAKE BREEZE
www.lakebreeze.com.au   (08) 8537 3017

LAMONTS
www.lamonts.com.au   (08) 9296 4485

LEAPING LIZARD (FERNGROVE)
www.ferngrove.com.au   (08) 9227 0297

LEASINGHAM (HARDY WINE COMPANY)
www.hardywines.com.au   (02) 9666 5855

LINDAUER (PERNOD RICARD)
www.pernod-ricard-pacific.com   1300 363 153

LINDEMANS (FOSTER'S)
www.fostersgroup.com   1300 651 650

LITTLE PENGUIN (FOSTER'S)
www.fostersgroup.com   1300 651 650
LITTLE REBEL
www.littlerebel.com.au   (03) 9739 0666
LOGAN
www.loganwines.com.au   (02) 6373 1333
LONG FLAT WINE CO (CHEVIOT BRIDGE)
www.cheviotbridge.com.au   (03) 9820 9080
MADFISH
www.madfishwines.com.au   (08) 9423 1200
MAJELLA
www.majellawines.com.au   (08) 8736 3055
MATTHEW LANG (FOSTER'S)
www.fostersgroup.com   1300 651 650
MAXWELL (ANGOVE'S)
www.angoves.com.au   (08) 8580 3100
MCGUIGAN (ICON BRANDS)
www.mcguiganwines.co.au   (02) 8345 6377
MCPHERSON
www.mcphersonwines.com   (02) 943 1644
MCWILLIAM'S
www.mcwilliams.com.au   1800 800 584
MILLBROOK
www.millbrookwinery.com.au   (08) 9525 5796
MINCHINBURY (FOSTER'S)
www.fostersgroup.com   1300 651 650
MITCHELTON
www.mitchelton.com.au   (03) 5736 2222
MONTANA (PERNOD RICARD)
www.pernod-ricard-pacific.com   1300 363 153
MONTES (DAN MURPHY'S)
www.danmurphys.com.au   1300 723 388
MOONDAH BROOK (HARDY WINE COMPANY)
www.hardywines.com.au   1800 088 711
MORRIS (PERNOD RICARD)
www.pernod-ricard-pacific.com   1300 363 153
MOUNT HURTLE (VINTAGE CELLARS)
www.vintagecellars.com.au   1300 366 084

MOUNTADAM
www.mountadam.com.au (08) 8564 1900

MT PLEASANT (MCWILLIAM'S)
www.mcwilliams.com.au 1800 800 584

MT RILEY (ANGOVE'S)
www.angoves.com.au (08) 8580 3100

MOUNT TRIO
mttrio@omninet.net.au (08) 9853 1136

MURRAY DARLING COLLECTION
www.murraydarlingcollection.com.au (03) 5026 1932

NEPENTHE
www.nepenthe.com.au (08) 8398 8888

NOBILO (HARDY WINE COMPANY)
www.hardywines.com.au 1800 088 711

NOVA (WESTEND)
www.westendestate.com (02) 6964 1506

NUGAN
www.nuganestate.com.au (02) 6962 1822

OAKWAY
www.oakwayestate.com.au (08) 9731 7141

OATLEY
www.oatleywines.com.au (02) 9433 3255

O'LEARY WALKER
www.olearywalkerwines.com (08) 8843 0022

OMNI (HARDY WINE COMPANY)
www.hardywines.com.au 1800 088 711

ORLANDO (PERNOD RICARD)
www.pernod-ricard-pacific.com 1300 363 153

PARKER
www.parkercoonawarraestate.com.au (08) 8737 3525

PARRI
www.parriestate.com.au (08) 8554 9595

PASCAL DELAUNAY (DAN MURPHY'S)
www.danmurphys.com.au 1300 723 388

PENFOLDS (FOSTER'S)
www.fostersgroup.com 1300 651 650

PENLEY
www.penley.com.au (08) 8363 5500

FINDING THE WINES   225

PETER LEHMANN
www.peterlehmannwines.com.au					(08) 8843 4370

PFEIFFER
www.pfeifferwines.com.au					(02) 6033 2805

PIRRAMIMMA
www.pirramimma.com.au					(08) 8323 8205

PLANTAGENET
www.plantagenetwines.com					(08) 9851 3111

POETS CORNER (PERNOD RICARD)
www.pernod-ricard-pacific.com					1300 363 153

PORTONE (VINTAGE CELLARS)
www.vintagecellars.com.au					1300 366 084

PREECE (MITCHELTON)
www.mitchelton.com.au					(03) 5736 2222

PRESTON VALE
www.prestonvale.com.au					(08) 9335 1166

PRIMO ESTATE
www.primoestate.com.au					(08) 8380 9442

PRINTHIE
www.printhiewines.com.au					(02) 6366 8422

PUNT ROAD
www.puntroadwines.com.au					(03) 9739 0666

QUEEN ADELAIDE (FOSTER'S)
www.fostersgroup.com					1300 651 650

REDBANK (NEGOCIANTS)
www.negociantsaustralia.com					(08) 8112 4210

RED KNOT (SHINGLEBACK)
www.shingleback.com.au					(08) 8370 2299

RENMANO (HARDY WINE COMPANY)
www.hardywines.com.au					(02) 9666 5855

REX WATSON (WATSON WINE GROUP)
www.wwgwines.com					(08) 8338 3200

RICCADONNA (FOSTER'S)
www.fostersgroup.com					1300 651 650

ROSEMOUNT ESTATE (FOSTER'S)
www.fostersgroup.com					1300 651 650

ROUGE HOMME (FOSTER'S)
www.fostersgroup.com					1300 651 650

RUFFINO (VINTAGE CELLARS)
www.vintagecellars.com.au   1300 366 084

RUTHERGLEN ESTATES
cellar@rutherglenestates.com.au   (02) 6032 8516

SALTRAM (FOSTER'S)
www.fostersgroup.com   1300 651 650

SANDALFORD
www.sandalford.com   (08) 9374 9374

SATELLITE (DAN MURPHY'S)
www.danmurphys.com.au   1300 723 388

SCARPANTONI
www.scarpontoni-wines.com.au   (08) 8383 0186

SCHILD
www.schildestate.com.au   (08) 8524 5560

SEGURA VIUDAS (BACARDI LION)
www.bacardilion.com.au   1800 357 994

SEPPELT (FOSTER'S)
www.fostersgroup.com   1300 651 650

SHAW & SMITH
www.shawandsmith.com   (08) 8398 0500

SIR JAMES (HARDY WINE COMPANY)
www.hardywines.com.au   (02) 9666 5855

SIRROMET
www.sirromet.com   (07) 3206 2999

SKUTTLEBUTT (STELLA BELLA)
www.stellabella.com.au   (08) 9757 6377

SQUITCHY LANE
www.squitchylane.com.au   (03) 5964 9114

STANLEY (HARDY WINE COMPANY)
www.hardywines.com.au   (02) 9666 5855

STANTON & KILLEEN
www.stantonandkilleenwines.com.au   (02) 6032 9457

STARVEDOG LANE (HARDY WINE COMPANY)
www.hardywines.com.au   (02) 9666 5855

STELLA BELLA
www.stellabella.com.au   (08) 9757 6377

STICKS
www.sticks.com.au   (03) 9739 0666

STONELEIGH (PERNOD RICARD)
www.pernod-ricard-pacific.com　　　　　　　　1300 363 153

STONES (ANGOVE'S)
www.angoves.com.au　　　　　　　　(08) 8580 3100

STONY PEAK (FOSTER'S)
www.fostersgroup.com　　　　　　　　1300 651 650

SUNNYVALE (ICON BRANDS)
www.mirandawines.com.au　　　　　　　　(02) 8345 6307

SWEET ANGELINA (ALL SAINTS)
www.allsaintswine.com.au　　　　　　　　(02) 6035 2222

SWEET NICOLI (ALL SAINTS)
www.allsaintswine.com.au　　　　　　　　(02) 6035 2222

TAHBILK
www.tahbilk.com.au　　　　　　　　(03) 5794 2555

TALIJANCICH
www.taliwine.com.au　　　　　　　　(08) 9296 4289

TALTARNI
www.taltarni.com.au　　　　　　　　(03) 5459 7923

TAMINICK
www.taminickcellars.com.au　　　　　　　　(03) 5766 2282

TANGLED VINE (VINTAGE CELLARS)
www.vintagecellars.com.au　　　　　　　　1300 366 084

TARRAWARRA
www.tarrawarra.com.au　　　　　　　　(03) 5957 3504

TATACHILLA (FINE WINE PARTNERS)
www.finewinepartners.com　　　　　　　　1300 668 512

TAYLORS
www.taylorswines.com.au　　　　　　　　(08) 8849 2008

TELMO RODRIGUEZ (SPANISH ACQUISITION)
tsa@thespanishacquisition.com　　　　　　　　(03) 9495 6373

T'GALLANT (FOSTER'S)
www.fostersgroup.com　　　　　　　　1800 007 282

TIM ADAMS
www.timadamswines.com.au　　　　　　　　(08) 8842 2429

TOBACCO ROAD (VICTORIAN ALPS)
www.victorianalpswinery.com　　　　　　　　(03) 5751 1992

TOLLANA (FOSTER'S)
www.fostersgroup.com　　　　　　　　1300 651650

TORBRECK
www.torbreck.com   (08) 8562 4155

TORRES (NEGOCIANTS)
www.negociantsaustralia.com   (08) 8112 4210

TRENTHAM ESTATE
www.trenthamestate.com.au   (03) 5024 8888

TULLOCH (ANGOVE'S)
www.angoves.com.au   (08) 8580 3100

TWO HANDS
www.twohandswines.com   (08) 8367 0555

TYRRELL'S
www.tyrrells.com.au   (02) 9889 4450

VINO GUSTO (VINTAGE CELLARS)
www.vintagecellars.com.au   1300 366 084

VINTAGE CELLARS
www.vintagecellars.com.au   1300 366 084

WAIRAU RIVER
www.liquidlibrary.net.au   (08) 9321 5522

WATERSHED
www.watershedwines.com.au   (08) 9758 8633

WATER WHEEL
www.waterwheelwine.com   (03) 5437 3060

WERE
www.wereestate.com.au   (08) 6389 1217

WEST CAPE HOWE
www.wchowe.com.au   (08) 9388 9994

WESTEND
www.westendestate.com   (02) 6964 1506

WILLOW BRIDGE
www.willowbridge.com.au   (08) 9728 0055

WINDANCE
www.windance.com.au   (08) 9755 2293

WIRRA WIRRA
www.wirrawirra.com   (08) 8112 4210

WOLF BLASS (FOSTER'S)
www.fostersgroup.com   1300 651 650

WOODSTOCK
www.woodstockwine.com.au   (08) 8383 0156

WYNDHAM ESTATE (PERNOD RICARD)
www.pernod-ricard-pacific.com   1300 363153

X & Y (MCWILLIAM'S)
www.mcwilliams.com.au   1800 800 584

XABREGAS
www.xabregas.com.au   (08) 9321 2366

XANADU
www.xanaduwines.com   (08) 9757 2581

YALUMBA
www.yalumba.com   (08) 8112 4200

YARRA BURN (HARDY WINE COMPANY)
www.hardywines.com.au   (02) 9666 5855

YELLOWGLEN (FOSTER'S)
www.fostersgroup.com   1300 651 650

YELLOW TAIL (CASELLA)
www.casellawines.com.au   (02) 6961 3000

ZEMA
www.zema.com.au   (08) 8736 3219

ZILZIE
www.zilziewines.com   (03) 9417 1966

ZONTE'S FOOTSTEP
www.zontesfootstep.com.au   (08) 8537 3334

Recommended Retailers

Again, making friends with a good bottleshop is the best way to gain direct access to the great bargains – the one-offs and specials as well as the wines from small producers that haven't yet become cult buys (and are therefore unobtainable). This list has been put together by combining our own experience of various bottleshops around the country, and asking a network of contacts, including wine producers, wholesalers and distributors, where the best places to buy wine are located.

NATIONAL

Because of their size (between them they control about 40% of the market – and this percentage is growing), the Coles Myer and Woolworths stores often have the best prices, but they can lack range and depth of wines on offer.

Coles Myer – Liquorland, Vintage Cellars, Quaffers, Theo's
For store locations: 1300 366 084
www.vintagecellars.com.au

Woolworths – Safeway & Woolworths Liquor Stores, Dan Murphy's, BWS
For store locations: www.woolworths.com.au

The following group of wine merchants was formed to counter the power of the supermarket chains by working collaboratively while remaining independent.

The Alliance of Fine Wine Merchants
For store locations: www.thewinealliance.com

The following group of independent stores uses the marketing strength of the group to compete with the supermarket chains.

Cellarbrations
For store locations: www.cellarbrations.com.au

NEW SOUTH WALES
SYDNEY

Amato's Liquor Mart
267-277 Norton Street, Leichhardt, NSW 2040
(02) 9560 7628
amatos@amatos.com.au

Annandale Cellars
119 Johnston Street, Annandale, NSW 2038
(02) 9660 1947
sales@annandalecellars.com.au

Avalon Fine Wine and Foods
35 Avalon Parade, Avalon, NSW 2107
(02) 9918 3207
www.avalonfinewine.com.au

Best Cellars
91 Crown Street, East Sydney, NSW 2010
(02) 9361 3733
www.bestcellars.com.au

Camperdown Cellars
140-144 Parramatta Road, Camperdown, NSW 2050
(02) 9517 2000

City Cellars
54 Lime Street, Sydney, NSW 2000
(02) 9299 3385
www.citycellars.com.au
sales@citycellars.com.au

Dee Why Hotel
834 Pittwater Road (cnr Sturdee Parade), Dee Why, NSW 2099
(02) 9981 1166
afeild@afeildhotels.com.au

Five Ways Cellars
4 Heeley Street, Paddington, NSW 2021
(02) 9360 4242
iancook@fivewaycellars.com.au

Jim's Cellars
65 Edgeworth David Avenue, Waitara, NSW 2077
(02) 9489 7177
www.jimscellars.com

Kemenys
137 Bondi Road, Bondi, NSW 2026
13 8881
www.kemenys.com.au

Liquor Brothers
3a Anella Avenue, Castle Hill, NSW 2154
(02) 9680 7311

Newport Bottler
386 Barrenjoey Road, Newport, NSW 2106
(02) 9997 6721

North Sydney Cellars
MLC Building, Shop 4, 105 Miller Street, North Sydney, NSW 2060
(02) 9954 0090
www.northsydneycellars.com.au

Palm Beach Wine Co.
1109 Barrenjoey Road, Palm Beach, NSW 2108
(02) 9974 4304
www.palmbeachwineco.com
sales@palmbeachwineco.com

Polifroni Cellars
Shop 1/169 Annangrove Road, Annangrove, NSW 2156
(02) 9679 0144

Porters Liquor
For store locations: www.portersliquor.com.au
(02) 9816 3044

Ultimo Wine Centre
21/99 Jones Street, Ultimo, NSW 2007
(02) 9211 2380
www.ultimowinecentre.com.au

OUTSIDE SYDNEY

Elanora Hotel
41 Victoria Street, Gosford East, NSW 2250
(02) 4325 2026
www.elanorahotel.com.au

Lambton Fridge
86 Elder Street, Lambton, NSW 2299
(02) 4957 1274

Leura Cellars
169-171 Leura Mall, Leura, NSW 2780
(02) 4784 1122

Oxford Tavern
47 Crown Street, Wollongong, NSW 2500
(02) 4228 3892
www.oxford-tavern.com.au
info@oxford-tavern.com.au

Toowoon Bay Cellars
153-155 Bay Road, Toowoon Bay, NSW 2261
(02) 4332 7459

Tosti Cellars
136 Wentworth Street, Port Kembla, NSW 2505
(02) 4274 1315
www.tosticellars.com.au

VICTORIA

MELBOURNE

6J's Wine Merchants
Shop 814, Prahran Market, 163 Commercial Road, South Yarra, VIC 3141
(03) 9824 2751
www.6js.com.au

Armadale Cellars
813-817 High Street, Armadale, VIC 3143
(03) 9509 3055
www.armadalecellars.com.au

City Wine Shop
159–161 Spring Street, Melbourne, VIC 3000
(03) 9654 6657
www.citywineshop.net.au

Cloudwine Cellars
317 Clarendon Street, South Melbourne, VIC 3205
(03) 9699 6700
766 Burke Road, Camberwell, VIC 3124
(03) 9882 0954
Dendy Plaza, 34 Church Street, Brighton, VIC 3002
(03) 9553 8416
www.cloudwine.com.au

Europa Cellars
Shop G3/150 Wellington Parade, East Melbourne, VIC 3002
(03) 9417 7220
www.europacellars.com.au
wine@europacellars.com.au

King & Godfree
293 Lygon Street, Carlton, VIC 3053
(03) 9347 1619
kgodfree@aol.com

McCoppins
165 Johnston Street, Fitzroy, VIC 3065
(03) 9417 5089
mccoppins-fitzroy@iinet.net.au

Parkhill Cellars
43–45 Errol Street, North Melbourne, VIC 3051
(03) 9328 1132
www.parkhillcellars.com

Prince Wine Store
177 Bank Street, South Melbourne VIC 3205
(03) 9686 3033
2a Acland Street, St Kilda, VIC 3182
(03) 9536 1155
www.princewinestore.com

Randall's
   186 Bridport Street, Albert Park, VIC 3206
   (03) 9686 4122
   www.randalls.net.au

Rathdowne Cellars
   348 Rathdowne Street, Carlton North, VIC 3054
   (03) 9349 3366
   www.rathdownecellars.com.au

Winebins
   58 Commercial Road, Prahran, VIC 3181
   (03) 9510 5424

OUTSIDE MELBOURNE

Bannockburn Cellars
   150 Pakington Street, Geelong West, VIC 3218
   (03) 5229 5358
   www.bannockburncellars.com.au

Corky's Liquor
   2-6 Breed Street, Traralgon, VIC 3844
   (03) 5174 1211
   www.corkys.com.au
   admin@corkys.com.au

International Fine Wines
   Building 38, Lionel Street, Essendon Airport, VIC 3041
   (03) 9379 0803
   www.ifw.com.au
   orders@ifw.com.au

Jack's Wine and Spirits
   901 Sturt Street, Ballarat, VIC 3350
   (03) 5332 1176
   www.jackswine.com.au

K.M. Lynch
   116-118 Fairy Street, Warrnambool, VIC 3280
   (03) 5562 4939

Murray Esplanade Cellars
2 Lesley Street, Echuca, VIC 3564
(03) 5482 6058
mecellars@ozemail.com.au

Neuschafers
90 Mercer Street, Geelong, VIC 3220
(03) 5229 8871

Randall the Wine Merchant
324 Pakington Street, Newtown, VIC 3220
(03) 5223 1141
www.randalls.net.au
newton@randall.net.au

SOUTH AUSTRALIA

ADELAIDE

East End Cellars
22–26 Vardon Avenue, Adelaide, SA 5000
(08) 8232 5300
www.eastendcellars.com.au
wine@eastendcellars.com.au

Edinburgh Cellars
7 High Street, Mitcham, SA 5062
(08) 8373 2753
www.edinburgh.com.au
cellars@edinburgh.com.au

Fassina Liquor Merchants
37–39 Oaklands Road, Somerton Park, SA 5044
(08) 8376 1848
admin@fassina.com.au

Goodwood Cellars
125 Goodwood Road, Goodwood SA 5034
(08) 8271 7481
goodwoodcellars@toucangroup.com.au
www.goodwoodcellars.com

Melbourne Street Cellars
93 Melbourne Street, North Adelaide, SA 5006
(08) 8267 1533
ms93@tpg.com.au

Norwood Hotel
97 The Parade, Norwood, SA 5067
(08) 8431 1822

Parade Cellars
Shop 15, Norwood Place, 161-175 The Parade, Norwood, SA 5067
(08) 8332 0317
paradecellars@optusnet.com.au

Royal Oak Hotel
123 O'Connell Street, North Adelaide, SA 5006
(08) 8267 2488

Wine ground
121 Pirie Street, Adelaide, SA 5000
(08) 8232 1222
www.wineunderground.com.au

OUTSIDE ADELAIDE

Berri Resort Hotel
Riverview Drive, Berri, SA 5342
(08) 8582 1411
www.berriresorthotel.com
ontheriver@berrirestorhotel.com

Fidler & Webb
60-66 Commercial Street East, Mt Gambier, SA 5290
(08) 8725 3038
fidwebb@datafast.net.au

Grand Tasman Hotel
94 Tasman Terrace, Port Lincoln, SA 5606
(08) 8682 2133
gthotel@internide.on.net
www.grandhotel.com.au

QUEENSLAND
BRISBANE

1st Choice Liquor
Jindalee Hotel, Sinnamon Road (cnr Goggs Road), Jindalee QLD 4074
(07) 3710 5858
(manager) carly.milnthorpe@coles.com.au

1st Choice Liquor
577 Settlement Road, Keperra, QLD 4054
(07) 3351 0499
www.1stchoice.com.au

Cru Bar & Cellar
22 James Street, Fortitude Valley, QLD 4006
(07) 3252 1744
www.crubar.com

The Gap Tavern
21 Glenquarie Place, The Gap, QLD 4061
(07) 3366 6090
www.gaptavern.com.au

Paddington Tavern
186 Given Terrace, Paddington, QLD 4064
(07) 3369 0044
www.maguireshotels.com.au

Stewarts Wine Co.
Racecourse Road (cnr Dobson Street), Ascot, QLD 4007
1300 138 838
www.stewartswineco.com.au

Story Bridge Hotel
200 Main Street, Kangaroo Point, QLD 4169
(07) 3391 2266
www.storybridgehotel.com.au
reception@storybridgehotel.com.au

Vintage Cellars
85 Merthyr Road, New Farm, QLD 4005
(07) 3358 6000
www.vintagecellars.com.au

RECOMMENDED RETAILERS

The Wine Emporium
Shop 47, 1000 Ann Street, Fortitude Valley QLD 4006
(07) 3252 1117
www.thewineemporium.com.au
thevalley@thewineemporium.com.au

Wine@era
102 Melbourne Street, South Brisbane QLD 4101
(07) 3832 4722
www.erabistro.com.au

OUTSIDE BRISBANE

1st Choice Liquor
201 Ferry Road, Southport, QLD 4215
(07) 5556 5155

Austral Hotel
189 Victoria Street, Mackay, QLD 4740
(07) 4951 3288
www.australhotel.com.au

Barrier Reef Hotel
33 Wharf Street, Cairns, QLD 4870
(07) 4051 4245

Courthouse Hotel
51 Nerang Street, Southport, QLD 4215
(07) 5532 0122
www.courthousehotel.com

Seaview Hotel
56 The Strand, North Ward, QLD 4810
(07) 4771 5005
seaview@pubzco.com.au

Smithfield Tavern
Captain Cook Highway, Smithfield, QLD 4878
(07) 4038 1411

Sunshine Cellars
50 Hastings Street, Noosa Heads, QLD 4567
(07) 5447 5166

Villa Noosa Hotel
Mary Street, Noosaville, QLD 4566
(07) 5430 5555
www.villanoosa.com.au

WESTERN AUSTRALIA
PERTH

Barossa Cellars
278 Railway Parade, Leederville, WA 6007
(08) 9381 1770

Bicton Cellars
221 Preston Point Road, Bicton, WA 6157
(08) 9339 1917
www.bictoncellars.com.au

BWS
Shop 1/22 Culloton Crescent, Balga, WA 6061
(08) 9342 2568
www.beerwinespirit.com.au

Chateau Guildford
124 Swan Street, Guildford, WA 6055
(08) 9377 3311

Grant & Knowles
24 Railway Street, Cottesloe, WA 6011
(08) 9384 3920

Harborne & Cambridge Cellars
252 Cambridge Street, Wembley, WA 6014
(08) 9388 3033
enquiries@hc-wines.com.au

Invinity Fine Wine Brokers
Level 1/58 Kishorn Rd, Mt Pleasant, WA 6153
(08) 9315 3777
www.invinity.com.au
kenr@invinity.com.au

RECOMMENDED RETAILERS 241

La Vigna
 302 Walcott Street, Mt Lawley, WA 6050
 (08) 9271 1179
 www.lavigna.com.au
 lavigna@lavigna.com.au

Liquor Barons Herdsman
 Shop 5/1 Flynn Street, Churchlands, WA 6018
 (08) 9387 4222
 herdsman@liquorbarons.com.au

Liquor Barons Mt Lawley
 654 Beaufort Street, Mt Lawley, WA 6050
 (08) 9271 0886
 grandcru@oinet.net.au

Liquor Barons South Perth
 23 Mends Street, South Perth, WA 6050
 (08) 9367 1001
 southperth@liquorbarons.com.au

Old Bridge Cellars
 221 Queen Victoria Street, North Fremantle, WA 6159
 (08) 9335 2702
 oldbridge@iinet.net.au

Paddington Ale House
 141 Scarborough Beach Road, Mt Hawthorn, WA 6016
 (08) 9242 3077
 www.paddo.com.au
 info@paddo.com.au

Re Store
 231 Oxford Street, Leederville, WA 6007
 (08) 9444 9644
 admin@the-re-store.com.au

Re Store
 72 Lake Street, Northbridge, WA 6003
 (08) 9328 1877

Rossmoyne Cellars
 5 Third Avenue, Rossmoyne, WA 6148
 (08) 9457 6439

Scarborough Cellars
166 Scarborough Beach Road, Scarborough, WA 6019
(08) 9341 1437
scarcell@bigpond.com

Sexton Cellars
30 Sexton Road, Inglewood, WA 6052
(08) 9370 4111
ingewinestore@yahoo.com.au

Swanbourne Cellars
103 Claremont Crescent, Swanbourne, WA 6010
(08) 9384 2111
swanycellars@bigpond.com

ACT

1st Choice Liquor Superstore
170 Melrose Drive, Phillip, ACT 2606
(02) 6122 8900
www.1stchoice.com.au

Australian Winebrokers
21 Lonsdale Street, Braddon, ACT 2612
(02) 6262 8599
www.australianwinebrokers.com

Braddon Cellars
11 Lonsdale Street, Braddon ACT
(02} 6247 2440

Campbell's Liquor Discount
4 Blamey Place, Campbell, ACT 2612
(02) 6247 1366

George's Liquor Stable
17 Dundas Court, Phillip, ACT 2606
(02) 6285 3075

Jim Murphy's Market Wine Cellars
19 Mildura Street, Fyshwick, ACT 2609
(02) 6295 0060
jcellars@bigpond.net.au

Local Liquor
1 Wattle Place, Lyneham, ACT 2602
(02) 6249 7263
www.localliquor.com.au

The Wine Shed
Shop 27, Belconnen Markets, Lathlain Street, Belconnen, ACT 2617
(02) 6 251 3781
wineshed@grapevine.com.au

TASMANIA
HOBART
Aberfeldy Cellars BWS
124 Davey Street, Hobart, TAS 7000
(03) 6211 6633
www.beerwinespirit.com.au

Gasworks 9/11 Bottleshop
Shop 3/2 Macquarie Street, Hobart, TAS 7000
(03) 6214 7525
bwiggers@vantagegroup.com.au

OUTSIDE HOBART
Alexander Hotel
79 Formby Road, Devonport, TAS 7310
(03) 6424 2671
sbraddey@goodstone.com.au

Benchmark Tasmania Wine Gallery
135 Paterson Street, Launceston, TAS 7250
(03) 6331 3977
www.benchmarkwinegallery.com
info@pineaushop.com

Club Hotel
22 Mount Street, Burnie, TAS 7320
(03) 6432 3666

Gunners Arms Tavern
23 Lawrence Street, Launceston, TAS 7250
(03) 6331 3891

HOW TO TRACK DOWN THE BARGAINS

TRC Bottleshop
131 Paterson Street, Launceston, TAS 7250
(03) 6331 3424
trc@bigpond.com

NORTHERN TERRITORY

Beachfront Hotel
342 Casuarina Drive, Rapid Creek, NT 0810
(08) 8985 3000
beachfront@hotkey.net.au

Hidden Valley Tavern
644 Stuart Highway, Berrimah, NT 0828
(08) 8984 3999
info@hiddenvalleytavern.com.au

Northside Foodland
3 Hearn Place, Alice Springs, NT 0870
(08) 8952 2754
north@venturin.com.au

Parap Fine Foods
40 Parap Road, Parap, NT 0820
(08) 8981 8597
www.parapfinefoods.com
Neville@parapfinefoods.com

Parap Village Tavern
15 Parap Road, Parap, NT 0820
(08) 8981 2191
parapvillagetavern@bigpond.com

Vintage Cellars
27 Cavenagh Street, Darwin, NT 0800
(08) 8941 7345
www.vintagecellars.com.au

WINE CLUBS AND ONLINE RETAILERS

There are disadvantages to joining a direct-selling wine club like Cellarmasters or The Wine Society – the main ones being the inability to try before you buy, and the fact that you have to take the rough with the smooth: not every wine you are sent will be a masterpiece of the vintner's art (that's one way that costs are kept so low). The same applies to buying wine over the internet.

WINE CLUBS

Cellarmasters
1800 500 260
www.cellarmasters.com.au

Liquorland Direct
1300 300 640
www.liquorlanddirect.com.au

Vintage Cellars
1300 366 084
www.vintagecellars.com.au

Wine Selectors
1300 303 307
www.wineselectors.com.au

The Wine Society
1300 723 723
www.winesociety.com.au

ONLINE STORES

The following websites often have some excellent prices, and all have a good range, including some smaller-producer, harder-to-get wines and, in many cases, a wide range of cleanskins.

www.auscellardoor.com.au
www.auswine.com.au
www.boccaccio.com.au
www.boutiquewineries.com.au
www.ckdirect.com.au
www.cleanskins.com
www.discountwines.com
www.nicks.com.au
www.organicwine.com.au
www.ozliquormart.com.au
www.prospectwines.com.au
www.tastingromm.com.au
www.winelarder.com.au
www.winepool.com.au
www.winestar.com.au
www.winezy.com.au

SEARCH ENGINES

The Wine Searcher website is very powerful and extremely useful in finding wines – and their wildly varying prices – all around the world, not just in Australia. If you buy a lot of wine online, it's worth signing up to the Pro version:

www.wine-searcher.com

And despite its limited scope, the Wine Robot search engine can return some great bargains:

www.winerobot.com.au

Decoding the jargon
A quick wine glossary

A QUICK WINE GLOSSARY

MAX ALLEN

aromatic
A catch-all phrase that refers to wines with strong positive aromas, such as the powerfully varietal smells of good sauvignon blanc.

austere
A wine that tastes a little mean, hard and tight, as though the flavours are there, but the wine doesn't want to give them to you.

bottle-aged
If wines are left alone in the bottle for a number of years, they can develop complex, savoury bottle-aged characters, quite distinct from the fresh, fruity characters they had when they were young.

buttery
Some winemaking techniques – for example, malolactic fermentation and lees contact – can contribute a rich, creamy, buttery aroma and flavour to wooded whites such as chardonnay.

chalky
Steely, flinty, minerally. The words used to describe really dry white wines.

chewy
Chewy red wines have lots of grape-skin extracts in them, giving a strong impression of being really thick and full in the mouth.

clean
Simply, a wine that is free of faults: fresh-tasting, pleasant. 'Clean' can occasionally be a more loaded description, implying that the wine is technically correct, but not overly exciting.

closed
Or dumb. A wine that tastes like a shadow of its former self. The opposite, of course, is 'open' or 'forward': a wine that seems to be wearing all its flavours on its sleeve and showing off a bit.

coarse
Wine that's a bit unsubtle and rough-tasting is 'coarse' – a bit too dry, a bit too sharp. 'Unbalanced' might be more correct; 'rustic' might be more diplomatic.

complex
You take a sniff and smell blackberries. You take another sniff and smell cherries. Another and wet undergrowth. Another and just a hint of fresh cracked pepper. This is a complex wine.

dusty
The tannins in young red wines can give a bizarre impression of being dry and dusty along the sides and back of your tongue.

elegant
A word you see a lot on wine labels. It means exactly what it says: the wine is balanced, tastes fine, is pleasing – all without knocking your tastebuds around.

fat
A wine that fills every corner of your mouth and sits plumply, but perhaps a little clumsily, on your tongue.

faults
Things can go wrong with wine at any stage, from when the grapes are picked to when the bottle is opened. The symptoms and causes of the most common faults are listed below. If you find them in your wine, you have every right to complain, send back the bottle to the waiter, or ask for an exchange from the bottleshop.

fault 1: hazy appearance
In wines that should be crystal clear – like young riesling, for example – cloudiness can indicate bacterial spoilage.

fault 2: dull, brown colour

The wine has come into contact with too much oxygen due to a leaky cork, has oxidised and is on its way to becoming vinegar. This is more relevant for white wine.

fault 3: musty, mouldy smells

Occasionally caused by the wine being stored in dirty, old barrels, but most often a musty smell is caused by cork taint. Cork is prone to all kinds of contamination that can, in turn, taint the wine, making it taste 'corked' – flat, dull, even quite rank – like mouldy cardboard.

fault 4: smells like rotten eggs or burnt matches

Rotten eggs is hydrogen sulphide, which can form in a wine during fermentation. It is usually easily dealt with by the winemaker, but occasionally creeps into the bottle. Burnt match smells are due to excessive sulphur dioxide, which is a preservative added to most wines.

fault 5: vinegary or solvent smells

These come from excessive levels of volatile acids (known as VA), and/or ethyl acetate. The volatile acids (such as the vinegar acid, acetic acid) are the ones we can smell. Ethyl acetate is formed when acetic acid combines with alcohol. A little VA can add complexity and lift the aromas of a wine; a lot can make it smell like nail-polish remover.

'fault' 6: tiny, crunchy crystals in the bottle

You can come across these in sweet white wines and older red wines. They are *not a fault*, but natural tartrate crystals that can develop when the wine ages or gets too cold. They do not affect the wine's taste or quality.

finish

The aftertaste. As in: 'This full-bodied shiraz has an extraordinarily long finish that lingers in the mouth for a minute.' As with so much else in life, the longer the better, obviously.

firm

Solid, taut, tense, sturdy – a more pleasant version of 'austere'.

fleshy

A more positive way of saying 'fat': a wine with plenty of palpable fruit in the mouth.

floral

Literally smelling like flowers.

full-bodied

A wine that fills the mouth and seems to impose on the palate – in contrast with medium- and light-bodied wines, which make a less imposing impression.

green or herbaceous

There are two main reasons why a wine might smell grassy, herbaceous or green. It's either meant to – like sauvignon blanc – or the grapes that made it were underripe – like some red wines grown in very cool climates.

hot

Wine made from overripe grapes grown in warm climates can produce a hot-tasting burn of alcohol at the back of the throat. The fruit in those wines can also taste a bit jammy.

lifted

Sometimes the delicate, spicy or fragrant aromas in a wine seem to be lifted towards your nose by some invisible hand.

long

A very good thing. A wine that has a long finish is one whose flavours seem to go on and on and on for seconds, right down the back of your throat.

nose

How the wine smells. As in: 'This young chardonnay has a marvellous nose of apples, vanilla and oatmeal.' If you're feeling posh, you could use the word 'bouquet'.

nutty

Sometimes wines can taste nutty because of the barrels they're stored in (chardonnay, for example), and sometimes it's a flavour found in the grape variety they're made from (pinot gris).

oaky or woody
Again, a catch-all term that covers all sorts of descriptions from the vanilla-like smell of new oak barrels used to age the wine before bottling to the cedarwood smell of old cabernet, and also covering the toasty smells, the spicy smells, the dusty smells and even the dirty old barrel smells.

rich
Wine with lots of viscosity, flesh, substance and fruit.

smoky
Some white grapes such as gewürztraminer and pinot gris can make wines with a dusky, smoky perfume; and sometimes barrels can give wine that's stored in them a different, more pungent, smoky or charred aroma.

spicy
Like smoky aromas, spicy characters can come from the grape varieties – the pepperiness of shiraz, for example – or the barrel – the clove and aniseed aromas of some (French) oak.

stalky
A little stalkiness (in wines that have been fermented with a few of the grape stems included) can be a good, complex thing. A lot just makes the wine taste green and stalky.

tannic
Tannins are the astringent bit of grape skins. Grapes with thick skins and lots of tannin such as cabernet can produce 'tannic' wine, which tastes particularly dry and savoury, like the liquid is gripping onto your tongue and gums before you swallow.

thin
The opposite of fat, and hardly ever a good thing. Thin wines, wines that are really neutral-tasting, that seem hollow and lean, are usually the result of overcropped grapes and poor winemaking.

varietal
Literally, 'tastes like the grape variety the wine was made from'.

zingy
Crisp, fresh, lively, juicy, tangy, zesty, lemony, citrusy – these are all good words for wines with noticeable but pleasant acidity. 'Sharp' and 'sour' are used when the acid is unbalanced and unpleasant.

Index of wines

INDEX

A mano Fiano Greco 173
Ad Hoc 'Straw Man' Sauvignon Blanc Semillon 187
Adams Tim Botrytis Riesling 209
Alasia Moscato d'Asti 171
Alkoomi Semillon Sauvignon Blanc 85
Alkoomi Unwooded Chardonnay 53
All Saints Rutherglen Muscat 209
All Saints Rutherglen Tokay 209
All Saints 'The Keep' Golden Cream Sherry 164
Altano 181
Angas Brut 36
Angove's 'Bookmark' Marsala 166
Angove's 'Bookmark' Cream Sherry 164
Angove's 'Bookmark' Dry Sherry 164
Angove's 'Bookmark' Medium Sherry 164
Angove's 'Bookmark' Sweet Sherry 164
Angove's 'Bookmark' Tawny Port 161
Angove's 'Butterfly Ridge' Colombard Chardonnay 92
Angove's Fortified Shiraz 162
Angoves 'Long Row' Cabernet Sauvignon 108
Angove's 'Long Row' Chardonnay 55
Angove's 'Long Row' Riesling 64
Angove's 'Long Row' Sauvignon Blanc 69
Angove's 'Long Row' Shiraz 127
Angove's 'Long Row' Verdelho 78
Angove's 'Nine Vines' Grenache Shiraz Rose 99
Angove's 'Nine Vines' Shiraz Viognier 124
Angove's 'Nine Vines' Viognier 76
Angove's 'Red Belly Black' Shiraz 120
Angove's 'Stonegate' Petit Verdot 131
Angove's 'Vineyard Select' Riesling 62
Anvers 'Brabo' Cabernet Shiraz 145
Anvers Semillon Sauvignon Blanc 84
Arrogant Frog Syrah Rose 177

Back Vintage Chardonnay 59
Back Vintage Eden Valley Riesling 64
Baily & Baily Cabernet Sauvignon 112
Banrock Station Cabernet Merlot 26
Banrock Station Chardonnay 20
Banrock Station 'Reserve' Sparkling Shiraz 42
Banrock Station Semillon Chardonnay 21
Banrock Station Shiraz Cabernet 145
Banrock Station Sparkling Pinot Noir Chardonnay 36
Banrock Station Sparkling White Shiraz 41
Barking Owl Semillon Sauvignon Blanc 85
Barry Jim Watervale Riesling 62
Bay of Fires Gewürztraminer 187
Bay of Fires 'Tigress' Pinot Noir Chardonnay 186
Bay of Fires 'Tigress' Rosé 197
Belgravia Chardonnay 187
Bella Ridge Cabernet Shiraz 198
Bella Ridge Tempranillo 198

Beresford 'Highwood' Shiraz 120
Bethany Riesling 64
Bimbadgen Shiraz 198
Black Chook Sparkling Shiraz 43
Bleasdale Malbec 131
Bleasdale Shiraz Cabernet 146
Bleasdale Sparkling Shiraz 42
Borie de Maurel 'Esprit d'Automne' 179
Bowen Estate Cabernet Sauvignon 198
Braided River Pinot Noir 181
Braided River Sauvignon Blanc 175
Brookland Valley 'Verse 1' Rosé 197
Brown Brothers Dolcetto Syrah 155
Brown Brothers 'Everton' Chardonnay Sauvignon Blanc Pinot Gris 92
Brown Brothers Lexia 154
Brown Brothers Moscato 45
Brown Brothers Orange Muscat & Flora 156
Brown Brothers Vermentino 188
Brown Brothers 'Zibibbo' 44

Campbell's Classic Muscat 209
Campbell's Rutherglen Tokay 210
Canti Chardonnay Pinot Grigio 176
Capel Vale 'Debut' Cabernet Merlot 136
Capel Vale 'Debut' Chenin Blanc 76
Capel Vale 'Debut' Merlot 116
Capel Vale 'Debut' Pinot Noir 132
Capel Vale 'Debut' Sauvignon Blanc Semillon 85
Capel Vale 'Debut' Shiraz 124
Card Collection Chardonnay 57
Catching Thieves Semillon Sauvignon Blanc 84
Chalk Hill Moscato 46
Chalk Hill 'Sidetrack' Shiraz Cabernet Sauvignon Grenache 150
Chambers Muscadelle (Tokay) 165
Chandon Brut 186
Charles Melton Rose of Virginia 197
Clairault Sauvignon Blanc 188
Clos Petit Bellane Cotes du Rhone 179
Cockatoo Ridge Brut Cuvee 39
Cockatoo Ridge Sparkling Rosé 41
Coldstone Brut 37
Coldstone Tempranillo 133
Coldstream Hills Chardonnay 188
Commissioners Block Sauvignon Blanc 69
Commissioners Block Viognier 79
Concha Y Toro 'Casillero del Diablo' Cabernet 181
Concha Y Toro 'Casillero del Diablo' Merlot 182
Concha Y Toro 'Casillero del Diablo' Pinot Noir 179
Concha Y Toro 'Casillero del Diablo' Sauvignon Blanc 176
Concha Y Toro 'Casillero del Diablo' Shiraz 181
Concha Y Toro 'Casillero del Diablo' Shiraz Rosé 177

INDEX

Cookoothama Cabernet Merlot 137
Cookoothama Riesling 63
Cookoothama Shiraz 127
Coriole Chenin Blanc 92
Coriole 'Contour 4' Sangiovese Shiraz 149
Coriole Fiano 188
Coriole 'Redstone' Cabernet Merlot 137
Coriole Sangiovese 199
Corte Giara Pinot Grigio delle Venezie 176
Cross Country Crisp Dry White 22
Cumulus 'Climbing' Cabernet Sauvignon 199
Cumulus 'Climbing' Pinot Gris 189
Cumulus 'Rolling' Chardonnay 189

D'Arenberg 'D'Arry's Original' Shiraz Grenache 199
D'Arenberg Noble Chardonnay Semillon 209
D'Arenberg 'The Last Ditch' Viognier 189
D'Arenberg 'The Stump Jump' Grenache Shiraz Mourvedre 141
De Bortoli 8 Year Old Tawny Port 163
De Bortoli 'Deen Vat 1' Durif 131
De Bortoli 'Deen Vat 2' Sauvignon Blanc 69
De Bortoli 'Deen Vat 4' Petit Verdot 132
De Bortoli 'Deen Vat 5' Botrytis Semillon 156
De Bortoli 'Deen Vat 7' Chardonnay 57
De Bortoli 'Deen Vat 8' Shiraz 128
De Bortoli 'Deen Vat 9' Cabernet Sauvignon 110
De Bortoli 'Montage' Semillon Sauvignon Blanc 82
De Bortoli 'Premium' Liqueur Muscat 28
De Bortoli 'Premium Reserve' Merlot 26
De Bortoli 'Premium Reserve' Shiraz 25
De Bortoli 'Premium' Traminer Riesling 21
De Bortoli 'Sacred Hill' Cabernet Merlot 137
De Bortoli 'Sacred Hill' Semillon Chardonnay 92
De Bortoli 'Sacred Hill' Traminer Riesling 92
De Bortoli 'Sacred Hill' Unwooded Colombard Chardonnay 92
De Bortoli Semillon Sauvignon Blanc 22
De Bortoli 'Sero' Cabernet Rosato 99
De Bortoli 'Sero' Chardonnay Pinot Grigio 90
De Bortoli 'Sero' Syrah Tempranillo 149
De Bortoli Show Liqueur Muscat 165
De Bortoli 'Vittorio' Spumante 45
De Bortoli 'Wild Vine' Shiraz 124
De Bortoli 'Windy Peak' Chardonnay 55
De Bortoli 'Windy Peak' Pinot Noir 2006 131
De Bortoli 'Windy Peak' Pinot Noir 2007 132
De Bortoli 'Windy Peak' Sangiovese 132
De Bortoli 'Windy Peak' Sauvignon Blanc Semillon 86
De Bortoli 'Windy Peak' Shiraz 124
Deakin Estate Brut 39
Deakin Estate Cabernet Sauvignon 108
Deakin Estate Sauvignon Blanc 68
Deakin Estate Shiraz 127
Devil's Lair 'Fifth Leg' Chardonnay 55
Drylands Pinot Noir 180
Duboeuf Georges Chiroubles 200

Earthworks Cabernet Sauvignon 110
Earthworks Shiraz 124
Edwards Chardonnay 190
Edwards Semillon Sauvignon Blanc 190
Evans & Tate Chardonnay 190
Evans & Tate Margaret River Cabernet Merlot 200

Faber Petit Verdot 200
Ferngrove Chardonnay 190
Ferngrove 'Majestic' Cabernet Sauvignon 200
Ferngrove 'Symbols' Cabernet Merlot 136
Ferngrove 'Symbols' Sauvignon Blanc Semillon 82
Fire Gully Chardonnay 190
Firestick Semillon Sauvignon Blanc 82
Fishbone Merlot 116
Fishbone Shiraz 125
Fishbone 'Sweetlips' Late Harvest Verdelho 154
Flagstone 'Cellarhand' Chenin Blanc 176
Forester Cabernet Merlot 200
Four Sisters Chardonnay 57
Four Sisters Merlot 117
Four Sisters Sauvignon Blanc Semillon 82
Fox Creek 'Shadows Run' Chardonnay 58
Framingham Sauvignon Blanc 173
Frankland Estate 'Cooladerra' Riesling 191
Frankland Estate 'Isolation Ridge' Riesling 191
Frankland Estate 'Poison Hill' Riesling 191
Freeman Rondinella Corvina 201
Freixenet Brut Rosé 172
Freixenet 'Cordon Negro' Cava 171

Gemtree 'Citrine' Chardonnay 59
Gemtree 'Tadpole' Chardonnay Viognier 91
Gemtree 'Tadpole' Shiraz Cabernet 146
Geoff Merrill 'Jacko's Blend' Shiraz 202
Georges Duboeuf Chiroubles 200
Giesen Sauvignon Blanc 173
Gnangara Cabernet Merlot 138
Gnangara Chardonnay 55
Gnangara Sauvignon Blanc 67
Gnangara Shiraz 125
Golden Gate Medium Dry White 22
Gramps Shiraz 120
Grant Burge 'Barossa Vines' Chardonnay 56
Growers 'Peppermint Grove' Sauvignon Blanc Semillon 83
Growers 'Peppermint Grove' Unwooded Chardonnay 54

256 INDEX

Hanging Rock 'Rock' Semillon Sauvignon Blanc 83
Hardys 'Nottage Hill' Cabernet Shiraz 145
Hardys 'Reserve' Cabernet Sauvignon 25
Hardys 'Reserve' Chardonnay 20
Hardys 'Reserve' Shiraz 25
Hardys Tawny 28
Haselgrove 'MVS' Chardonnay 56
Haselgrove 'Sovereign Series' Chardonnay 59
Haselgrove 'Sovereign Series' Semillon Sauvignon Blanc 86
Heartland Cabernet Sauvignon 201
Heggies 'Reserve' Riesling 191
Henry Fessy 'Domaine des 40 Ecus' Beaujolais Villages 180
Henschke 'Eleanor's Cottage' Sauvignon Blanc Semillon 191
Houghton White Classic 90
Hugel 'Gentil' 173
Hugh Hamilton 'The Ruffian' Liqueur Muscat 210
Hungerford Hill Tumbarumba Chardonnay 192

Illuminati 'Campirosa' Montepulciano d'Abruzzo 182
Innocent Bystander Moscato 44
Irvine Albarino 192

Jacob's Creek Chardonnay Pinot Noir 39
Jacob's Creek 'Reserve' Cabernet Sauvignon 110
Jacob's Creek 'Reserve' Chardonnay 56
Jacob's Creek 'Reserve' Shiraz 125
Jacob's Creek Shiraz 128
Jacob's Creek 'Three Vines' Shiraz Cabernet Tempranillo 150
Jacob's Creek 'Three Vines' Shiraz Grenache Sangiovese 99
Jane Brook 'Plain Jane' Chardonnay Chenin Blanc 93
Jean Pierre Brut 39
Jim Barry Watervale Riesling 62

Kaesler 'Stonehorse' Shiraz 201
Kaiser Stuhl Rosé 24
Keith Tulloch Chardonnay 196
Killawarra Brut 37
Kingston 'Empiric' Petit Verdot 201
Kirrihill 'Companions' Cabernet Merlot 138
Kirrihill 'Companions' Shiraz Viognier 125
Knappstein Semillon Sauvignon Blanc 192
Koonara 'Angel's Peak' Cabernet Sauvignon 108

Lachlan Ridge Semillon Sauvignon Blanc 22
Lachlan Ridge Shiraz Cabernet 26
Lamont's Shiraz 202
Leaping Lizard Semillon Sauvignon Blanc 86

Leaping Lizard Shiraz 128
Leasingham 'Circa 1893' Chardonnay 56
Leasingham 'Circa 1893' Riesling 62
Leasingham 'Circa 1893' Shiraz Cabernet 145
Leasingham 'Magnus' Cabernet Sauvignon 112
Leasingham 'Magnus' Riesling 64
Leasingham 'Magnus' Sparkling Shiraz 43
Lehmann Peter Barossa Riesling 64
Lehmann Peter Barossa Shiraz Grenache 141
Lehmann Peter Cabernet Merlot 202
Lehmann Peter Chenin Blanc 77
Lehmann Peter 'Clancy's' Shiraz Cabernet Merlot 150
Lehmann Peter Eden Valley Riesling 2006 64
Lehmann Peter Eden Valley Riesling 2007 63
Lehmann Peter Semillon 72
Lehmann Peter Semillon Chardonnay 92
Lehmann Peter Shiraz Grenache 143
Lindauer Brut 172
Lindauer Special Reserve 172
Lindemans 'Bin 45' Cabernet Sauvignon 112
Lindemans 'Bin 50' Shiraz 128
Lindemans 'Bin 55' Shiraz Cabernet 145
Lindemans 'Cawarra' Shiraz Cabernet 146
Lindemans 'Cellar Choice' Crisp Dry White 22
Lindemans 'Cellar Choice' Soft Fruity White 21
Lindemans Reserve Cabernet Merlot 136
Lindemans Reserve Merlot 117
Little Penguin Merlot 117
Little Penguin Shiraz 125
Little Rebel Chardonnay 58
Logan 'Apple Tree Flat' Chardonnay 58
Logan 'Apple Tree Flat' Merlot 116
Logan 'Apple Tree Flat' Semillon Sauvignon Blanc 86
Logan 'Hannah' Rosé 197
Logan 'Weemala' Pinot Gris 76
Logan 'Weemala' Pinot Noir 133
Logan 'Weemala' Riesling 63
Long Flat 'Destinations' Chardonnay 58
Long Flat 'Destinations' Riesling 63
Long Flat 'Destinations' Sauvignon Blanc 67
Long Flat 'Destinations' Shiraz 121
Long Flat Moscato 45
Long Flat Semillon Sauvignon Blanc 22
Long Flat Shiraz 125
Longhop Shiraz 121

Mad Fish Riesling 192
Majella Cabernet Sauvignon 202
Majella 'The Musician' Cabernet Shiraz 202
Matthew Lang Brut Cuvee 37

INDEX

Maxwell Liqueur Mead 166
Maxwell Spiced Mead 166
McGuigan 'Bin 9000' Semillon 72
McPherson Cabernet Rosé 101
McWilliam's 'Hanwood' Cabernet Sauvignon 112
McWilliam's 'Hanwood' Chardonnay 59
McWilliam's 'Hanwood' Classic Tawny 162
McWilliam's 'Hanwood' Merlot 117
McWilliam's 'Hanwood' Pinot Noir Chardonnay 39
McWilliam's 'Hanwood' Shiraz 126
McWilliam's 'Hanwood' Verdelho 78
McWilliam's 'Inheritance' Cabernet Merlot 137
McWilliam's 'Inheritance' Semillon Sauvignon Blanc 86
McWilliam's 'Inheritance' Shiraz Merlot 150
McWilliam's 'Premium Selection' Tawny 29
Melton Charles Rose of Virginia 197
Merrill Geoff 'Jacko's Blend' Shiraz 202
Millbrook Viognier 193
Minchinbury Brut 39
Minchinbury White Seal 36
Mitchelton 'Blackwood Park' Riesling 193
Mitchelton Shiraz 203
Montana East Coast Rosé 177
Montana Sauvignon Blanc 174
Montes 'Classic Series' Sauvignon Blanc 176
Moondah Brook Rosé 99
Moondah Brook Verdelho 76
Morris 'Black Label' Liqueur Muscat 165
Morris 'Black Label' Old Tawny Port 161
Morris Classic Muscat 210
Morris Premium Dry White 22
Morris Tawny Port 29
Mount Hurtle Grenache Rosé 100
Mount Hurtle Grenache Shiraz Mourvedre 141
Mount Langi Ghiran 'Billi Billi' Shiraz 126
Mount Pleasant 'Elizabeth' Semillon 194
Mount Riley Pinot Noir 182
Mount Riley Sauvignon Blanc 174
Mount Trio Cabernet Merlot 137
Mount Trio 'Gravel Pit' Shiraz Viognier 203
Mountadam Riesling 193
Murray Darling Collection 'Murray Cod' Vermentino 193

Nepenthe 'Tryst' Cabernet Sauvignon Tempranillo Zinfandel 203
Nepenthe 'Tryst' Pinot Noir Chardonnay 38
Nobilo Merlot 182
Norfolk Rise Shiraz 126
Nova Moscato 45

Oakway Unwooded Chardonnay 54
Oatley 'Wild Oats' Shiraz Viognier 203
O'Leary Walker 'Blue Cutting Road' Cabernet Merlot 138

O'Leary Walker 'Blue Cutting Road' Sauvignon Blanc Semillon 84
O'Leary Walker 'Polish Hill River' Riesling 194
Omni Blue 44
Omni Citrus 45
Omni Pink 41
Omni Red 43
Orlando 'Trilogy' Pinot Noir Chardonnay Pinot Meunier 40

Parker 'Terra Rossa' Cabernet Sauvignon 204
Parri Viognier Chardonnay 91
Pascal Delaunay Val de Loire Rosé d'Anjou 178
Penfolds 'Club Reserve' Aged Tawny 161
Penfolds Club Tawny 163
Penfolds 'Koonunga Hill' Cabernet Sauvignon 111
Penfolds 'Koonunga Hill' Shiraz 121
Penfolds 'Rawsons Retreat' Cabernet Sauvignon 111
Penfolds 'Rawsons Retreat' Semillon Chardonnay 93
Penfolds 'Wood Aged' Muscat 28
Penfolds 'Wood Aged' Port 29
Penley Estate 'Condor' Shiraz Cabernet 204
Penley Estate 'Gryphon' Merlot 204
Penley Estate 'Phoenix' Cabernet Sauvignon 204
Peter Lehmann Barossa Riesling 64
Peter Lehmann Barossa Shiraz Grenache 141
Peter Lehmann Cabernet Merlot 202
Peter Lehmann Chenin Blanc 78
Peter Lehmann 'Clancy's' Shiraz Cabernet Merlot 152
Peter Lehmann Eden Valley Riesling 2006 64
Peter Lehmann Eden Valley Riesling 2007 63
Peter Lehmann Semillon 72
Peter Lehmann Semillon Chardonnay 92
Peter Lehmann Shiraz Grenache 143
Pfeiffer Classic Tokay 210
Pfeiffer Rutherglen Tokay 210
Pirramimma 'Pirra' Sparkling Chardonnay 38
Pirramimma 'Stocks Hill' Shiraz 204
Plantagenet 'Eros' Rosé 197
Plantagenet 'Hazard Hill' Semillon Sauvignon Blanc 85
Plantagenet 'Hazard Hill' Shiraz 126
Plantagenet Riesling 194
Poet's Corner Semillon Sauvignon Blanc 86
Portone Soave 175
Portone Valpolicella 180
Preece Cabernet Sauvignon 2005 109
Preece Cabernet Sauvignon 2006 112

Preece Merlot 116
Preece Shiraz 128
Preece Sparkling 40
Preece 'White Label' Chardonnay 58
Preston Vale Unwooded Chardonnay 54
Primo Estate 'Il Briccone' Shiraz Sangiovese 205
Primo Estate 'La Biondina' Colombard Sauvignon Blanc 91
Printhie Sauvignon Blanc 67
Punt Road Shiraz 205

Queen Adelaide Brut 40
Queen Adelaide Semillon Chardonnay 93

Red Knot Shiraz 122
Redbank 'Long Paddock' Shiraz 128
Renmano 'Premium Varietal' Semillon Sauvignon Blanc Chardonnay 21
Renmano 'Premium Varietal' Shiraz Cabernet Merlot 26
Rex Watson Cabernet Sauvignon 109
Rex Watson Shiraz 123
Rex Watson Unwooded Chardonnay 54
Riccadonna Asti 171
Richmond Grove 'Black Cat' Shiraz 126
Rockbare 'Mojo' Shiraz 122
Rosemount Estate 'Diamond Cellars' Cabernet Merlot 138
Rosemount Estate 'Diamond Cellars' Semillon Chardonnay 93
Rosemount Estate 'Diamond Cellars' Shiraz Cabernet 145
Rosemount Estate 'Diamond Label' Chardonnay 57
Rosemount Estate 'Diamond Label' Shiraz 122
Rouge Homme Cabernet Merlot 138
Ruffino 'Lumina' Pinot Grigio 175
Ruffino Rosa di Ninfa 178
Rutherglen Estate Durif 205

Saltram 'Maker's Table' Cabernet Sauvignon 113
Sandalford 'Element' Cabernet Sauvignon 111
Sandalford 'Element' Classic White 91
Sandalford 'Element' Merlot 117
Sandalford 'Protege' Chardonnay 194
Sandalford 'Protege' Rosé 100
Scarpantoni 'Ceres' Rosé 101
Scarpantoni Sauvignon Blanc 69
Schild Estate Grenache Mataro Shiraz 141
Segura Viudas Brut Reserva Cava 171
Seppelt 'DP 30' Trafford Tawny 161
Seppelt 'DP 33' Muscat 166
Seppelt 'DP 37' Tokay 166
Seppelt 'DP 63' Grand Muscat 210
Seppelt 'Moyston' Cabernet Merlot 205
Seppelt 'Solero' Extra Dry Sherry 28

Seppelt 'Solero' Sweet Sherry 29
Shaw & Smith Sauvignon Blanc 195
Shaw & Smith Shiraz 206
Sir James 36
Sirromet '820 Above' Rosé 100
Skuttlebutt Sauvignon Blanc Semillon 85
Squitchy Lane Chardonnay 195
Stanley Premium Tawny 28
Stanton & Killeen Classic Muscat 211
Stanton & Killeen Classic Tokay 211
Starvedog Lane Chardonnay Pinot Noir Pinot Meunier 186
Stella Bella Semillon Sauvignon Blanc 195
Sticks Chardonnay Viognier 93
Sticks Shiraz Viognier 122
Stoneleigh Pinot Noir 180
Stoneleigh Sauvignon Blanc 176
Stony Peak Shiraz Cabernet 146
Sunnyvale Dry White 21
Sunnyvale Medium Dry Red 27
Sweet Angelina 154
Sweet Nicoli 101

Tahbilk Marsanne 78
Tahbilk Riesling 64
Tahbilk Viognier 195
Talijancich 'Julian James' Red Liqueur 211
Taltarni 'T Series' Chardonnay Pinot Noir Pinot Meunier 38
Taminick Cellars Gold Port 162
Taminick Cellars Liqueur Muscat 162
Taminick Cellars 'Premium' Shiraz 206
Tangled Vine Fresh Dry White 22
Tangled Vine Soft Fruity White 23
Tarrawarra 'Tin Cows' Pinot Noir 206
Tatachilla Cabernet Sauvignon 207
Tatachilla 'Growers' Semillon Sauvignon Blanc 83
Taylors 'Jaraman' Riesling 196
Telmo Rodriguez Basa Verdejo 174
T'Gallant 'Juliet' Pinot Grigio 79
Tim Adams Botrytis Riesling 209
Tobacco Road Cabernet Sauvignon 111
Torbreck 'Woodcutters' Semillon 73
Torres 'De Casta Rosado 177
Torres 'Vina Esmeralda' 175
Trentham Estate Cabernet Merlot 138
Trentham Estate 'La Famiglia' Moscato 46
Trentham Estate 'La Famiglia' Pinot Grigio 77
Trentham Estate 'La Famiglia' Sangiovese Rosé 101
Trentham Estate Merlot 117
Trentham Estate 'Murphy's Lore' Chardonnay 59
Trentham Estate 'Murphy's Lore' Shiraz Cabernet 146
Trentham Estate 'Murphy's Lore' Autumn Red 155
Trentham Estate Noble Taminga 156

INDEX

Trentham Estate Pinot Noir 132
Trentham Estate 'Two Thirds' Semillon Sauvignon Blanc 86
Tulloch Cuvee Brut 38
Tulloch Keith Chardonnay 196
Tulloch Semillon 72
Tulloch Semillon Sauvignon Blanc 87
Two Hands 'Brilliant Disguise' Moscato 44
Tyrrell's 'Old Winery' Semillon 73
Tyrrell's 'Old Winery' Semillon Sauvignon Blanc 87
Tyrrell's 'Old Winery' Shiraz 128
Tyrrell's 'Old Winery' Verdelho 77

Vino Gusto Cabernet Merlot 137
Vino Gusto Semillon Sauvignon Blanc 87
Vintage Cellars (Barossa) Shiraz 123
Vintage Cellars Botrytis Semillon 156
Vintage Cellars Riesling 64
Vintage Cellars Sauvignon Blanc 68
Vintage Cellars Shiraz Viognier 128

Wairau River Sauvignon Blanc 196
Water Wheel 'Memsie' Shiraz Cabernet Malbec 149
Watershed 'Shades' Sauvignon Blanc Semillon 85
Watershed 'Shades' Sweet Margaret 155
Watershed 'Shades' Unwooded Chardonnay 54
Watson Rex Cabernet Sauvignon 109
Watson Rex Shiraz 123
Watson Rex Unwooded Chardonnay 54
Were Cabernet Sauvignon 207
West Cape Howe Cabernet Merlot 207
Westend 'Calabria' Saint Macaire 133
Westend Estate 'Outback' Cabernet Merlot 138
Westend 'Richland' Cabernet Merlot 136
Westend 'Richland' Pinot Grigio 77
Westend 'Richland' Sauvignon Blanc 68
Westend 'Richland' Shiraz 123
Willow Bridge Rosé 100
Willow Bridge Sauvignon Blanc Semillon 83
Willow Bridge Shiraz 127
Willow Bridge Shiraz Viognier 207
Willow Bridge Unwooded Chardonnay 53
Windance Semillon Sauvignon Blanc 196
Windance Shiraz 207
Wirra Wirra 'Mrs Wigley' Rosé 102
Wirra Wirra 'Scrubby Rise' Unwooded Chardonnay 53
Wolf Blass 'Eaglehawk' Cabernet Sauvignon 109
Wolf Blass 'Eaglehawk' Merlot 117
Wolf Blass 'Red Label' Chardonnay 58
Wolf Blass 'Red Label' Shiraz Grenache 142
Wolf Blass 'Red Label' Tawny Port 163
Wolf Blass 'Yellow Label' Shiraz 207
Woodstock Rosé 102
Woodstock Semillon Sauvignon Blanc 84
Wyndham Estate 'Bin 333' Pinot Noir 133
Wyndham Estate 'Bin 555' Sparkling Shiraz 42

X & Y Sauvignon Blanc 69
X & Y Chardonnay 59
Xabregas Show Reserve Chardonnay 196
Xanadu 'Dragon' Shiraz 127
Xanadu 'Dragon' Unwooded Chardonnay 53

Yalumba 'Bush Vine' Grenache 208
Yalumba Chardonnay 23
Yalumba Classic Dry Red 27
Yalumba Classic Dry White 23
Yalumba 'Dunes' Pinot Noir Chardonnay 40
Yalumba 'Mawson's' Cabernet Sauvignon 110
Yalumba 'Oxford Landing' Cabernet Shiraz 146
Yalumba 'Oxford Landing' Sauvignon Blanc 68
Yalumba 'Oxford Landing' Shiraz 128
Yalumba 'Reserve Selection' Cabernet Sauvignon 27
Yalumba 'Reserve Selection' Cabernet Merlot 26
Yalumba 'Reserve Selection' Merlot 25
Yalumba 'Reserve Selection' Rosé Shiraz 24
Yalumba 'Reserve Selection' Sauvignon Blanc Semillon 20
Yalumba 'Reserve Selection' Shiraz 27
Yalumba Riesling 21
Yalumba Spatlese Fruity White 23
Yalumba 'Y Series' Cabernet Sauvignon 111
Yalumba 'Y Series' Pinot Grigio 79
Yalumba 'Y Series' Sangiovese Rosé 100
Yalumba 'Y Series' Sauvignon Blanc 68
Yalumba 'Y Series' Shiraz 123
Yalumba 'Y Series' Shiraz Viognier 124
Yarra Burn Pinot Noir Chardonnay 186
Yarra Burn Pinot Noir Chardonnay Rosé 186
Yellow Tail Merlot 117
Yellowglen 'Bella' 46
Yellowglen 'Jewel' Pink 41
Yellowglen 'Jewel' Yellow 37
Yellowglen Pinot Noir Chardonnay 38
Yellowglen Red 43
Yellowglen Yellow 37

Zema 'Cluny' 208
Zilzie Cabernet Sauvignon 113
Zilzie Merlot 117
Zilzie Petit Verdot 133
Zilzie Pinot Grigio 78
Zilzie 'Selection 23' Sauvignon Blanc 69
Zonte's Footstep Cabernet Malbec 149

Now you can **Quaff** online!

The Quaffing experience doesn't have to end when you put this book down.

To receive weekly reviews of great-value wines throughout the year, **subscribe for free** at

www.quaff.com.au

and hear from us each Friday with our **Wine of the Week.**

We'll keep you informed throughout the year as the best wines under $15 hit the market.

Don't forget to tell your friends,

and **Quaff** on!